SOPHIA

The Journal of Traditional Studies

Special Issue 2009

SOPHIA is published bi-annually by The Foundation for Traditional Studies, a not-for-profit organization. Contributions are tax deductible to the extent of the law.

Subscription inquiries, changes of address, and all correspondence regarding editorial matters should be sent to:

The Foundation for Traditional Studies
P. O. Box 370
Oakton. VA 22124, USA

Phone: 703 476-8837 / Fax: 703 476-5218
E-mail: contactus@sophiajournal.com
Web: www.traditional-studies.org / www.sophiajournal.com

ISBN 978-0-9798429-8-4 / ISSN 1531 123

Cover: Conversation between Muslims and Christians. ca. 1595.
(Istanbul, Topkapi Museum, H. 3632, fol. 119b)

Table of Contents

Editorial Preface

A major and substantial step toward better Christian/Muslim relations was taken in 2008. The initiative, called *A Common Word Between Us and You*, began with a desire to create a pathway to peace through focusing the attention of leaders of the Islamic and Christian faiths, faiths whose adherents comprise over half of the world's population, on their shared values and beliefs—especially the love of God and the neighbor, rather than on their differences. (See www.acommonword.org for full details of this initiative.)

The vision that arose with this goal in mind quickly took a concrete shape. In October 2007 an Open Letter was written and signed by 138 Muslim scholars and intellectuals from the width and breadth of the Islamic world addressed to Christian Churches and denominations of the world inviting them to "come to a Common Word Between Us and You." Clearly the invitation was welcomed—the Christian response was profound. It echoed the Muslim call, and so began what has become a truly transformational dialogue whose effects are already carrying far beyond the walls of the conference rooms of the actual meetings of the representatives of the two religions.

Some of the major events of 2008 which followed upon the Open Letter included a conference at Yale University entitled "Loving God and Neighbor in Word and Deed," the "Conference on A Common Word and Future Muslim-Christian Engagement" at Cambridge University, and the "First Seminar of the Catholic-Muslim Forum" at the Vatican. From around the world, Christians have written significant responses to the Open Letter. HRH Ghazi bin Muhammad's speech (included in the issue) upon his acceptance of the 2008 Eugen Biser Award given to the initiative provides more details of the ongoing and future events and activities that are arising from this shared vision.

Thus far in 2009 we have witnessed, in addition to a growing stream of responses and lectures, "The Theory and Application of A Common Word" Symposium at the University of South Carolina in cooperation with Zayed University of the United Arab Emirates, and the historic visit of His Holiness Benedict XVI to Jordan.

Because of its exceptional significance, *Sophia* has chosen to celebrate this ongoing dialogue by printing several documents that have thus far become part of *A Common Word* initiative, including the original Open Letter. We have left them in their original formats. From the Open Letter that extended a hand of friendship, to papers from the Yale Conference, to addresses from the Vatican Conference, to the welcome address by HRH Ghazi bin Muhammad to His Holiness Benedict XVI on his journey to Jordan, all the writings herein resonate with the message of the call to "come to a common word" by addressing shared values and histories between Christianity and Islam and underscoring the urgent need for understanding between these great faiths.

Katherine O'Brien

A Common Word Between Us and You: Theological Motives and Expectations*

by Ghazi bin Muhammad

In the middle of the eastern Jordanian desert, in a place called Safawi, miles away from anything, from any landmark or any human traces, there stands a unique, solitary tree. This tree is around 1500 years old and there are no other trees to be seen for dozens of miles in any direction. Despite its age and breadth, it is only about 6-8 meters tall. It is a *butum* tree, a kind of pistachio tree that is found in our part of the world. I will come back to the significance of this tree in a few moments, God willing, but for now I want to say that it was in fact under this tree that *A Common Word* was born. For in September 2007, one month before the launch of *A Common Word*, I had the privilege to visit this tree twice, once in the company of a number of the scholars behind the *Common Word* initiative, and it was under this tree that we prayed to God (or at least I did) to grant *A Common Word* success.

I have been asked now to speak about *A Common Word Between Us and You*: Theological Motives and Expectations. So let me address these three elements in order, starting with an explanation and a review of *A Common Word Between Us and You*, then discussing the theological motives behind it, and finally revealing our expectations in issuing it.

A Common Word Between Us and You: A Review One Year On

Over the last year since the *A Common Word* initiative was launched, I do not think it is an exaggeration to say it has

* *This is the abridged text of the acceptance speech given on the occasion of the receipt of The Eugen Biser Award given to* A Common Word *in November 2008 in Germany.*

become the world's leading interfaith dialogue initiative between Christians and Muslims specifically. It was launched on October 13, 2007 initially as an open letter signed by 138 leading Muslim scholars and intellectuals (including such figures as the Grand Muftis of Egypt, Syria, Jordan, Oman, Bosnia, Russia and Istanbul) to the leaders of the Christian Churches and denominations of the entire world, including His Holiness Pope Benedict XVI. In essence it proposed, based on verses from the Holy Qur'an and the Holy Bible, that Islam and Christianity share, at their core, the twin "golden" commandments of the paramount importance of loving God and loving one's neighbor. Based on this joint common ground, it called for peace and harmony between Christians and Muslims worldwide.

Since its launch in October 2007, over 60 leading Christian figures gradually responded to it in one form or another, including His Holiness Pope Benedict XVI; His Beatitude Orthodox Patriarch Alexi II of Russia; Archbishop of Canterbury the Very Reverend Dr Rowan Williams,* and the head of the Lutheran World Federation, Bishop Mark Hanson (see: 'Christian Responses' at www.acommonword.com). In November 2007, over 300 leading US Evangelical leaders also responded to it in an open letter in the *New York Times,* and over the course of 2008 the Muslim scholars signing the initiative swelled to around 300, with over 460 Islamic organizations and associations also endorsing it. It has led to a number of spontaneous local grass-roots and community-level initiatives all over the world in places as far apart as India, Bangladesh, Canada, the USA, and Great Britain (see: 'New Fruits' at www.acommonword.com), and we keep hearing informal reports of other activities based upon it in various parts of the globe. It has been the subject of major international conferences at Yale University, and at Cambridge University and Lambeth Palace, and has been studied in such gatherings as the World Economic Forum in the Spring of 2008 and the Mediterranean Dialogue of Cultures in France in November 2008. It was also the basis for the historic First Annual Catholic-Muslim Forum held recently at the Vatican, in November 2008. Moreover, it was the central impetus of the Wamp-Ellison Resolution of 2008 in the U.S. House of Representatives. It

* *See this issue of* Sophia *for his full response.*

also received the UK's Association of Muslim Social Scientist 2008 Building Bridges Award, and today it receives the Eugen Biser Award of 2008.

There is an equal barrage of activity planned for 2009, including a major documentary film, three books that we know of so far (Yale, Georgetown and perhaps Oxford University Press); a joint Christian-Muslim sensitivity manual, an important political conference planned at Georgetown University, Washington DC; a large religious conference planned in Malaysia and possibly a third in the Philippines. Also planned are two high level meetings between Muslims and the Orthodox Churches, and between Muslims and the World Council of Churches; a multi-lingual Muslim-Christian 'recommended reading list' joint website with Yale, Lambeth Palace and possibly also the Vatican (to serve as a voluntary basis for school and university curricula); a Muslim Theological Press Conference in Spain; a major European-based global Christian-Muslim peace institute with *A Common Word* ensconced in its charter; a University campus-based *Common Word* student initiative in the USA; a joint-design *Common Word* Muslim-Christian string of prayer-beads; a number of 'trickledown' projects to try to bring the *Common Word* to churches and mosques all over the world; and finally the continuation of the practical work planned at the meetings in Yale, Cambridge/Lambeth Palace and the Vatican. In short, I think one may fairly say that in its first year *A Common Word* achieved—by the Grace of God, *al-hamdu li'Llāh*—historically unprecedented 'global traction', and is hoping in its second year—with the Will of God, *inshā'a'Llāh*—to achieve historically unprecedented 'global trickledown'. God is Bounteous! *Allāhu Karīm!*

The Theological Motives behind *A Common Word*

Exactly one month after His Holiness Pope Benedict XVI's controversial Regensburg lecture on September 13th 2006, an international group of 38 Muslim scholars and intellectuals issued an *Open Letter to His Holiness* in what we thought was a very gentle and polite way of pointing out some of His Holiness' factual mistakes in his lecture. We did not get a satisfactory answer from the Vatican beyond a perfunctory courtesy visit to me, a month later, from some Vatican officials. So exactly a year after our first letter (and a thus a year and a month after the Regensburg lecture) we increased our number by exactly 100, to 138, (symbolically saying that we are many and that we are not going away) and issued, based on the Holy Qur'an, *A Common Word between Us and You.* To ensure a more favorable response this time and to set the proper tone and appropriate momentum we hired a Public Relations firm and coordinated with a number of our important Christian friends to publicize some early positive Christian responses from them. This led, by the Grace of God, to all that I have just mentioned.

We had honestly—as is evident from the genesis of this story, and as is evident I believe in the very text of *A Common Word* itself—only one motive: peace. We were aiming to try to spread peace and harmony between Christians and Muslims all over the world, not through governments and treaties but on the all-important popular and mass level, through the world's most influential popular leaders precisely—that is to say through the leaders of the two religions. We wanted to stop the drumbeat of what we feared was a growing popular consensus (on both sides) for world-wide (and thus cataclysmic and perhaps apocalyptic) Muslim-Christian *jihād*/crusade. We were keenly aware, however, that peace efforts required also another element: knowledge. We thus aimed to spread proper basic knowledge of our religion in order to correct and abate the constant and unjust vilification of Islam, in the West especially.

I need hardly go over all the factors leading us to believe in a Muslim-Christian global 'Clash of Civilizations' since the collapse of the Soviet Union in 1990. These include: (1) Jerusalem and the Palestine question, (2) discontentment with US foreign policy (especially the war in Iraq), (3) terrorism, (4) fundamentalism and fundamentalist propaganda (on both sides), (5) missionary activity (also on both sides), and (6) deeply rooted, historical, cultural and racial, misunderstanding, suspicion and even loathing. Thus now, according to the results of the largest international religious surveys in history (as outlined in a recently-published seminal book by Professor John Esposito and Dalia Mogahed), 60% of Christians harbour prejudice against Muslims and 30% of Muslims reciprocate. Quite clearly the grounds for fear of war and religious genocides—as the Grand Mufti of Bosnia here today will personally attest—are starkly real.

Having said what our motive was, I want to emphasize what our motives *were not,* in view of some of the strange suspicions and speculations we have read about on the internet.

1. *A Common Word* was not intended—as some have misconstrued—to trick Christians or to foist Muslim theology on them, or even to convert them to Islam.

2. *A Common Word* was not intended to reduce both our religions to an artificial union based on the Two Commandments: indeed in Matthew 22:40 Jesus Christ the Messiah (*'alayhi 'l-salām*) was quite specific: "*On these two commandments <u>hang</u> all the Law and the Prophets.*" "*<u>Hang</u>*" not "are (reduced to)". It was simply an attempt to find a theologically correct pre-existing *essential* common ground (albeit interpreted perhaps differently) between Islam and Christianity, rooted in our sacred texts and in their common Abrahamic origin, in order to stop our deep-rooted religious mutual suspicions from being an impediment to behaving properly towards each other. It was, and is, an effort to ensure that religions behave as part of the solution, and are not misused to become part of the problem. Indeed, the Two Commandments give us guidelines and a concrete, shared standard of behaviour not only to what to expect from the other but also to how we must ourselves *behave* and *be.* We believe we can and must hold ourselves and each other to this shared standard.

3. *A Common Word* was not intended to deny that God loved us first, as some Christians have opined. The knowledge that God loved man before man loved God is so obvious in Islam that we did not think we had to make it explicit. It is obvious because God obviously existed before His creation of the world and man. It is also evident in the very sacred formula that starts every chapter in the Holy Qur'an but one, and that begins every single legitimate act of any Muslim's entire life—*Bismi 'Llāh al-Rahmān al-Rahīm* (In the Name of God, the Compassionate, the Merciful). Indeed, there is a *hadīth qudsi* (a 'holy saying'[1]), wherein

[1] *Sunan Al-Tirmithi*, no. 1907

God says that His Name is *al-Rahmān* (the Lovingly Compassionate) and that the word for 'womb' *(al-Rahm)* comes from His Name, and thus implying that God created the world out of an internal overflowing of love. Indeed, creation out of *Rahmah* (Loving Compassion) is also seen in the Holy Qur'an in beginning in the *Sura* of *al-Rahmān*, which says:

Al-Rahmān / Hath Taught the Quran / He hath created Man / He hath taught him speech. (*Al-Rahmān*, 55:1-4)

In other words, the very Divine Name *al-Rahmān* should be understood as containing the meaning of 'The Creator-through-Love', and the Divine Name *Al-Rahīm* should be understood as containing the meaning of 'The Saviour through Mercy'.

4. *A Common Word* was not intended to exclude Judaism as such or diminish from its importance. We started with Christianity bilaterally simply because Islam and Christianity are the two largest religions in the world and in history, and so in that sense, Islamic-Christian dialogue is the most critical: for there are about 2 billion Christians in the world and 1.5 billion Muslims and only 25 million Jews. But this does not preclude our having as Muslims other conversations with those of any other faith, bilaterally or multilaterally, or even with those of no faith at all. Moreover, Muslims do not object to the idea of a Judeo-Christian tradition (even though all 3 religions share the same Abrahamic origins and traditions), and do not object to not being invited to all the Jewish-Christian dialogues, so there is no need for Jews to feel excluded by a Muslim-Christian conversation. For that matter there is no need for Christians to feel excluded by a Judeo-Islamic dialogue. We can all, however, understand Jewish fears about this dialogue, and note that there have been Jewish observers invited to the conferences in Yale and Cambridge.

   On the other hand, I would like to say also that *A Common Word* does not signal that Muslims are prepared to deviate from or concede one iota of any their convictions in reaching out to Christians—nor, I expect, the opposite. Let us be crystal-clear: *A Common Word* is about equal peace, *not* about capitulation.

Indeed, some have suggested that framing our extended hand in the language of 'love' is such a concession, but I assure you that this is not at all accurate, nor is it a 'concession': rather, it has been a particular pleasure to be able to focus in our initiative on this frequently underestimated aspect of our religion: the Grand Principle of Love. Indeed, we have over 50 near-synonyms for love in the Holy Qur'an—English does not have the same linguistic riches and connotations. If Muslims do not usually use the same language of love as Christians in English, it is perhaps because the word 'love' for Muslims frequently implies different things for Muslims than it does Christians.

Our use of the language of 'love' in *A Common Word* is simply then a recognition that human beings have the same souls everywhere—however corrupted or pure—and thus that the experience of love must have something in common everywhere, even if the objects of love are different, and even if the ultimate love of God is stronger than all other loves. God says in the Holy Qur'an:

Yet of mankind are some who take unto themselves (objects of worship which they set as) rivals to God, loving them with a love like (that which is the due) of God (only)—[but] those who believe are stauncher in their love for God.... (*Al-Baqarah,* 2:165)

The Expectations behind *A Common Word*

Despite our prayers for success—in truth I remember praying to God to grant success beyond 'what can possibly be imagined' for the initiative—we had no expectations whatsoever, only some hope in God's generosity, and we were all resolved to accept a complete failure. This prayer itself was a gift from God, for it is not within man's power to achieve sincerity and detachment if God does not grant them to him—*with man this is impossible, with God all things are possible.* However, I have to say, Praise God, *al-hamdu li'Llāh*, that I am continually astonished by the spectacular way God has answered the prayer that was His gift in the first place. I suppose that is one of the great wonders of God's love for man: He rewards human beings for gifts he has given them in the first place. He keeps giving and giving, and all that He requires from us is to accept! *Subhan Allāh!* Glory be to God!

Now I want to return to the tree that I mentioned at the start of my talk, the tree under which prayers were offered for *A Common Word.* Despite today being in a completely desolate place, there lay until the last century not far from this tree the clear remains of an ancient Roman road and of a later but also ancient Byzantine monastery. And according to the earliest Islamic historical sources, some 1400 years ago, on one of the caravan roads from Arabia to Syria, a nine-year-old Meccan boy named Muhammad bin Abdullah from the clan of Hashem (may peace and blessing be upon him) traveled with his uncle Abu Talib to Syria from his home in Eastern Arabia. A cloud hung over him wherever he went, and when he sat under a tree in the desert, the tree too lowered its branches to shield him from the desert heat. A local Christian monk named Bahira noticed these two miracles from a little distance, and summoned the caravan and the boy, and after courteously examining and speaking to him, Bahira witnessed the boy as a future Prophet to his people. The monk had a book with him that led him to expect a Prophet among the Arabs, who were descended from Ishmael the eldest son of the Prophet Abraham (peace be upon him). Perhaps it was the Torah, for Genesis 49: 10 and Deuteronomy 18:15 seem to predict a prophet that is not the Messiah and not Judah but from the 'brethren' of the Jews, but we do not know. Howbeit, what is most important here is that the self-same blessed tree underneath which *A Common Word* was born, also itself gave rise, 1400 years ago to the first harmonious contact between the founder of Islam and Christianity! Indeed, it is immensely significant that God draws a direct analogy between a good word and a good tree (and both their fruits) in the Holy Qur'an as follows:

Seest thou not how God coineth a similitude: A good word is as a good tree, its root set firm, its branches in heaven, / Giving its fruit at every season by permission of its Lord? God coineth the similitudes for mankind in order that they may reflect. / And the similitude of a bad word is as a bad tree, uprooted from upon the ground, possessing no stability. / God confirmeth those who believe by a firm saying in the life of the world and in the Hereafter; and God sendeth wrong-doers astray. And God doeth what He will. (*Ibrahim,* 14:24-27)

بسم الله الرحمن الرحيم

In the Name of God, the Compassionate, the Merciful

A Common Word Between Us and You*

Muslims and Christians together make up well over half of the world's population. Without peace and justice between these two religious communities, there can be no meaningful peace in the world. The future of the world depends on peace between Muslims and Christians.

The basis for this peace and understanding already exists. It is part of the very foundational principles of both faiths: love of the One God, and love of the neighbour. These principles are found over and over again in the sacred texts of Islam and Christianity. The Unity of God, the necessity of love for Him, and the necessity of love of the neighbour is thus the common ground between Islam and Christianity. The following are only a few examples:

> Of God's Unity, God says in the Holy Qur'an: *Say: He is God, the One! / God, the Self-Sufficient Besought of all!* (*Al-Ikhlas*, 112:1-2). Of the necessity of love for God, God says in the Holy Qur'an: *So invoke the Name of thy Lord and devote thyself to Him with a complete devotion* (*Al-Muzzammil*, 73:8). Of the necessity of love for the neighbour, the Prophet Muhammad (*'alayhi 'l-salāt[u] wa 'l-salām*) said: "*None of you has faith until you love for your neighbour what you love for yourself.*"
>
> In the New Testament, Jesus Christ (*'alayhi 'l-salām*) said: *'Hear, O Israel, the Lord our God, the Lord is One. / And you shall love the Lord your God with all your heart, with all your soul, with all your mind, and with all your strength.'*

* *This is the Open Letter signed by 138 leading Muslim scholars and intellectuals and addressed to Christian Churches and denominations of the entire world.*

> *This is the first commandment. / And the second, like it, is this: 'You shall love your neighbour as yourself.' There is no other commandment greater than these."* (Mark 12:29-31)

In the Holy Qur'an, God Most High enjoins Muslims to issue the following call to Christians (and Jews—the *People of the Scripture*):

> *Say: O People of the Scripture! Come to a common word between us and you: that we shall worship none but God, and that we shall ascribe no partner unto Him, and that none of us shall take others for lords beside God. And if they turn away, then say: Bear witness that we are they who have surrendered (unto Him).* (*Aal 'Imran* 3:64)

The words: *we shall ascribe no partner unto Him* relate to the Unity of God, and the words: *worship none but God*, relate to being totally devoted to God. Hence they all relate to the *First and Greatest Commandment*. According to one of the oldest and most authoritative commentaries on the Holy Qur'an the words: *that none of us shall take others for lords beside God*, mean 'that none of us should obey the other in disobedience to what God has commanded'. This relates to the Second Commandment because justice and freedom of religion are a crucial part of love of the neighbour.

Thus in obedience to the Holy Qur'an, we as Muslims invite Christians to come together with us on the basis of what is common to us, which is also what is most essential to our faith and practice: the *Two Commandments* of love.

بسم الله الرحمن الرحيم

In the Name of God, the Compassionate, the Merciful,
Call unto the way of thy Lord with wisdom and fair exhortation, and contend with them in the fairest way. Lo! thy Lord is Best Aware of him who strayeth from His way, and He is Best Aware of those who go aright.

(The Holy Qur'an, *Al-Nahl*, 16:125)

(I) Love of God

Love of God in Islam

The Testimonies of Faith

The central creed of Islam consists of the two testimonies of faith or *Shahadahs*,[1] which state that: *There is no god but God, Muhammad is the messenger of God.* These Two Testimonies are the *sine qua non* of Islam. He or she who testifies to them is a Muslim; he or she who denies them is not a Muslim. Moreover, the Prophet Muhammad (*'alayhi 'l-salāt^u wa 'l-salām*) said: *The best remembrance is: 'There is no god but God' ....*[2]

The Best that All the Prophets have Said

Expanding on *the best remembrance*, the Prophet Muhammad (*'alayhi 'l-salāt^u wa 'l-salām*) also said: *The best that I have said—myself, and the prophets that came before me—is: 'There is no god but God, He Alone, He hath no associate, His is the sovereignty and His is the praise and He hath power over all things'.*[3] The phrases which follow the First Testimony of faith are all from the Holy Qur'an; each describe a mode of love of God, and devotion to Him.

The words: *He Alone*, remind Muslims that their hearts[4] must be

[1] In Arabic: *La illaha illa Allah Muhammad rasul Allah.* The two *Shahadahs* actually both occur (albeit separately) as phrases in the Holy Qur'an (in *Muhammad,* 47:19, and *Al-Fath,* 48:29, respectively).

[2] *Sunan Al-Tirmidhi, Kitab Al-Da'awat*, 462/5, no. 3383; *Sunan Ibn Majah*, 1249/2.

[3] *Sunan Al-Tirmidhi, Kitab Al-Da'awat, Bab al-Du'a fi Yawm 'Arafah, Hadith* no. 3934. It is important to note that the additional phrases, *He Alone, He hath no associate, His is the sovereignty and His is the praise and He hath power over all things*, all come from the Holy Qur'an, in exactly those forms, albeit in different passages. *He Alone*—referring to God Y—is found at least six times in the Holy Qur'an (7:70; 14:40; 39:45; 40:12; 40:84 and 60:4). *He hath no associate*, is found in exactly that form at least once (*Al-An'am*, 6:173). *His is the sovereignty and His is the praise and He hath power over all things*, is found in exactly this form once in the Holy Qur'an (*Al-Taghabun*, 64:1), and parts of it are found a number of other times (for instance, the words, *He hath power over all things*, are found at least five times: 5:120; 11:4; 30:50; 42:9 and 57:2).

[4] *The Heart*: In Islam the (spiritual, not physical) heart is the organ of perception of spiritual and metaphysical knowledge. Of one of the Prophet Muhammad's (*'alayhi 'l-salāt^u wa 'l-salām*) greatest visions God says in the Holy Qur'an: *The inner heart lied not (in seeing) what it saw.* (*al-Najm*, 53:11) Indeed, elsewhere in the Holy Qur'an, God says: *[F]or indeed it is not the eyes that grow blind, but it is the hearts, which are within the bosoms, that grow blind.* (*Al-Hajj*, 22:46; see

devoted to God Alone, since God says in the Holy Qur'an: *God hath not assigned unto any man two hearts within his body* (*Al-Ahzab*, 33:4). God is Absolute and therefore devotion to Him must be totally sincere.

The words: *He hath no associate*, remind Muslims that they must love God uniquely, without rivals within their souls, since God says in the Holy Qur'an: *Yet there are men who take rivals unto God: they love them as they should love God. But those of faith are more intense in their love for God ....* (*Al-Baqarah*, 2:165). Indeed, *[T]heir flesh and their hearts soften unto the remembrance of God ....* (*Al-Zumar*, 39:23).

The words: *His is the sovereignty*, remind Muslims that their minds or their understandings must be totally devoted to God, for *the sovereignty* is precisely everything in creation or existence and everything that the mind can know. And all is in God's Hand, since God says in the Holy Qur'an: *Blessed is He in Whose Hand is the sovereignty, and, He is Able to do all things* (*Al-Mulk*, 67:1).

The words: *His is the praise* remind Muslims that they must be grateful to God and trust Him with all their sentiments and emotions. God says in the Holy Qur'an:

> *And if thou wert to ask them: Who created the heavens and the earth, and constrained the sun and the moon (to their appointed work)? they would say: God. How then are they*

whole verse and also: 2:9-10; 2:74; 8:24; 26:88-89; 48:4; 83:14 et al.. There are in fact over a hundred mentions of the heart and its synonyms in the Holy Qur'an.)

Now there are different understandings amongst Muslims as regards the direct Vision of God (as opposed to spiritual realities as such) God, be it in this life or the next—God says in the Holy Qur'an (of the Day of Judgement): *That day will faces be resplendent, / Looking toward their Lord*; (*Al-Qiyamah*, 75:22-23) Yet God also says in the Holy Qur'an:

> *Such is God, your Lord. There is no God save Him, the Creator of all things, so worship Him. And He taketh care of all things. / Vision comprehendeth Him not, but He comprehendeth (all) vision. He is the Subtile, the Aware. / Proofs have come unto you from your Lord, so whoso seeth, it is for his own good, and whoso is blind is blind to his own hurt. And I am not a keeper over you.* (*Al-An'am*, 6:102-104)

Howbeit, it is evident that the Muslim conception of the (spiritual) heart is not very different from the Christian conception of the (spiritual) heart, as seen in Jesus's (*'alayhi 'l-salām*) words in the New Testament: *Blessed are the pure in heart, for they shall see God.* (Matthew 5:8); and Paul's words: *For now we see in a mirror, dimly, but then face to face. Now I know in part, but then I shall know just as I am known.* (1 Corinthians 13:12)

> *turned away ? / God maketh the provision wide for whom He will of His servants, and straiteneth it for whom (He will). Lo! God is Aware of all things. / And if thou wert to ask them: Who causeth water to come down from the sky, and therewith reviveth the earth after its death ? they verily would say: God. Say: Praise be to God! But most of them have no sense.* (*Al-'Ankabut*, 29:61-63)[5]

For all these bounties and more, human beings must always be truly grateful:

> *God is He Who created the heavens and the earth, and causeth water to descend from the sky, thereby producing fruits as food for you, and maketh the ships to be of service unto you, that they may run upon the sea at His command, and hath made of service unto you the rivers; / And maketh the sun and the moon, constant in their courses, to be of service unto you, and hath made of service unto you the night and the day./ And He giveth you of all ye ask of Him, and if ye would count the graces of God ye cannot reckon them. Lo! man is verily a wrong-doer, an ingrate.* (*Ibrahim*, 14:32-34)[6]

Indeed, the *Fatihah*—which is the *greatest chapter in the Holy Qur'an*[7]—starts with praise to God:

> *In the Name of God, the Infinitely Good, the All-Merciful. /*
> *Praise be to God, the Lord of the worlds. /*
> *The Infinitely Good, the All-Merciful. /"*
> *Owner of the Day of Judgement. /*
> *Thee we worship, and Thee we ask for help. /*
> *Guide us upon the straight path. /*
>
> *The path of those on whom is Thy Grace, not those who deserve anger nor those who are astray.* (*Al-Fatihah*, 1:1-7)

The *Fatihah*, recited at least seventeen times daily by Muslims in the canonical prayers, reminds us of the praise and gratitude due to God for His Attributes of Infinite Goodness and All-Mercifulness, not

[5] See also: *Luqman*, 31:25.

[6] See also: *Al-Nahl*, 16:3-18.

[7] *Sahih Bukhari, Kitab Tafsir Al-Qur'an, Bab ma Ja'a fi Fatihat Al-Kitab* (*Hadith* no.1); also: *Sahih Bukhari, Kitab Fada'il Al-Qur'an, Bab Fadl Fatihat Al-Kitab*, (*Hadith* no.9), no. 5006.

merely for His Goodness and Mercy to us in this life but ultimately, on the Day of Judgement[8] when it matters the most and when we hope to be forgiven for our sins. It thus ends with prayers for grace and guidance, so that we might attain—through what begins with praise and gratitude— salvation and *love*, for God says in the Holy Qur'an: *Lo! those who believe and do good works, the Infinitely Good will appoint for them love*. (*Maryam*, 19:96)

The words: *and He hath power over all things*, remind Muslims that they must be mindful of God's Omnipotence and thus fear God.[9] God says in the Holy Qur'an:

> ... *[A]nd fear God, and know that God is with the God-fearing. / Spend your wealth for the cause of God, and be not cast by your own hands to ruin; and do good. Lo! God loveth the virtuous. / ....* (*Al-Baqarah*, 2:194-5)...
>
> *[A]nd fear God, and know that God is severe in punishment.* (*Al-Baqarah*, 2:196)

Through fear of God, the actions, might and strength of Muslims should be totally devoted to God. God says in the Holy Qur'an:

> ...*[A]nd know that God is with those who fear Him.* (*Al-Tawbah*, 9:36) ....
>
> *O ye who believe! What aileth you that when it is said unto you: Go forth in the way of God, ye are bowed down to the ground with heaviness. Take ye pleasure in the life of the world rather than in the Hereafter? The comfort of the life of*

[8] The Prophet Muhammad (*'alayhi 'l-salāt[u] wa 'l-salām*) said: *God has one hundred mercies. He has sent down one of them between genii and human beings and beasts and animals and because of it they feel with each other; and through it they have mercy on each other; and through it, the wild animal feels for its offspring. And God has delayed ninety-nine mercies through which he will have mercy on his servants on the Day of Judgement.* (*Sahih Muslim, Kitab Al-Tawbah*; 2109/4; no. 2752; see also *Sahih Bukhari, Kitab Al-Riqaq*, no. 6469).

[9] *Fear of God is the Beginning of Wisdom:* The Prophet Muhammad (*'alayhi 'l-salāt[u] wa 'l-salām*) is reported to have said: *The chief part of wisdom is fear of God—be He exalted* (*Musnad al-Shahab*, 100/1; Al-Dulaymi, *Musnad Al-Firdaws*, 270/2; Al-Tirmidhi, *Nawadir Al-Usul*; 84/3; Al-Bayhaqi, *Al-Dala'il* and Al-Bayhaqi, *Al-Shu'ab*; Ibn Lal, *Al-Makarim*; Al-Ash'ari, *Al-Amthal*, et al.) This evidently is similar to the Prophet Solomon words in the Bible: The *fear of the LORD is the beginning of Wisdom ....* (Proverbs 9:10); and: *The fear of the LORD is the beginning of knowledge.* (Proverbs 1:7)

the world is but little in the Hereafter. / If ye go not forth He will afflict you with a painful doom, and will choose instead of you a folk other than you. Ye cannot harm Him at all. God is Able to do all things. (*Al-Tawbah*, 9:38-39)

The words: *His is the sovereignty and His is the praise and He hath power over all things*, when taken all together, remind Muslims that just as everything in creation glorifies God, everything that is in their souls must be devoted to God:

All that is in the heavens and all that is in the earth glorifieth God; His is the sovereignty and His is the praise and He hath power over all things. (*Al-Taghabun*, 64:1)

For indeed, all that is in people's souls is known, and accountable, to God:

He knoweth all that is in the heavens and the earth, and He knoweth what ye conceal and what ye publish. And God is Aware of what is in the breasts (of men). (*Al-Taghabun*, 64:4)

As we can see from all the passages quoted above, souls are depicted in the Holy Qur'an as having three main faculties: the mind or the intelligence, which is made for comprehending the truth; the will which is made for freedom of choice, and sentiment which is made for loving the good and the beautiful.[10] Put in another way, we could

[10] *The Intelligence, the Will and Sentiment in the Holy Qur'an*: Thus God in the Holy Qur'an tells human beings to believe in Him and call on Him (thereby using the intelligence) with fear (which motivates the will) and with hope (and thus with sentiment):

> *Only those believe in Our revelations who, when they are reminded of them, fall down prostrate and hymn the praise of their Lord, and they are not scornful, / Who forsake their beds to cry unto their Lord in fear and hope, and spend of that We have bestowed on them. / No soul knoweth what is kept hid for them of joy, as a reward for what they used to do.* (*Al-Sajdah*, 32:15-17)

> (*O mankind!*) *Call upon your Lord humbly and in secret. Lo! He loveth not aggressors. / Work not confusion in the earth after the fair ordering (thereof), and call on Him in fear and hope. Lo! the mercy of God is near unto the virtuous.* (*Al-A'raf*, 7:55-56)

Likewise, the Prophet Muhammad (*'alayhi 'l-salāt*[u] *wa 'l-salām*) himself is described in terms which manifest knowledge (and hence the intelligence), eliciting hope (and hence sentiment) and instilling fear (and hence motivating the will):

say that man's soul knows through *understanding* the truth, through *willing* the good, and through virtuous emotions and *feeling* love for God. Continuing in the same chapter of the Holy Qur'an (as that quoted above), God orders people to fear Him as much as possible, and to listen (and thus to understand the truth); to obey (and thus to will the good), and to spend (and thus to exercise love and virtue), which, He says, is better for our souls. By engaging *everything* in our souls—the faculties of knowledge, will, and love—we may come to be purified and attain ultimate success:

> *So fear God as best ye can, and listen, and obey, and spend; that is better for your souls. And those who are saved from the pettiness of their own souls, such are the successful.* (*Al-Taghabun*, 64:16)

In summary then, when the entire phrase *He Alone, He hath no associate, His is the sovereignty and His is the praise and He hath power over all things* is added to the testimony of faith—*There is no god but God*—it reminds Muslims that their hearts, their individual souls and all the faculties and powers of their souls (or simply their *entire* hearts and souls) must be totally devoted and attached to God. Thus God says to the Prophet Muhammad (*'alayhi 'l-salāt^u wa 'l-salām*) in the Holy Qur'an:

> *Say: Lo! my worship and my sacrifice and my living and my dying are for God, Lord of the Worlds. / He hath no partner. This am I commanded, and I am first of those who surrender (unto Him). / Say: Shall I seek another than God for Lord, when He is Lord of all things? Each soul earneth only on its own account, nor doth any laden bear another's load....* (*Al-An'am*, 6:162-164)

These verses epitomize the Prophet Muhammad's (*'alayhi 'l-salāt^u wa 'l-salām*) complete and utter devotion to God. Thus in the Holy Qur'an God enjoins Muslims who truly love God to follow this

O Prophet! Lo! We have sent thee as a witness and a bringer of good tidings and a warner. (*Al-Ahzab*, 33:45)
Lo! We have sent thee (O Muhammad) as a witness and a bearer of good tidings and a warner, (*Al-Fath*, 48:8)

example,[11] in order in turn to be loved[12] by God:

> *Say, (O Muhammad, to mankind): If ye love God, follow me; God will love you and forgive you your sins. God is Forgiving, Merciful.* (*Aal 'Imran*, 3:31)

Love of God in Islam is thus part of complete and total devotion to God; it is not a mere fleeting, partial emotion. As seen above, God commands in the Holy Qur'an: *Say: Lo! my worship and my sacrifice and my living and my dying are for God, Lord of the Worlds. / He hath no partner*. The call to be totally devoted and attached to God heart and soul, far from being a call for a mere emotion or for a mood, is in fact an injunction requiring all-embracing, constant and active love of God. It demands a love in which the innermost spiritual heart and the whole of the soul—with its intelligence, will and feeling—participate through devotion.

None Comes with Anything Better

We have seen how the blessed phrase: *There is no god but God, He Alone, He hath no associate, His is the sovereignty and His is the praise and He hath power over all things*—which is the best that all the prophets have said—makes explicit what is implicit in *the best remembrance* (*There is no god but God*) by showing what it requires and entails, by way of devotion. It remains to be said that this blessed formula is also in itself a sacred invocation—a kind of extension of the First Testimony of faith (*There is no god but God*)—the ritual repetition of which can bring about, through God's grace, some of

[11] *A Goodly Example:* The love and total devotion of the Prophet Muhammad (*'alayhi 'l-salāt[u] wa 'l-salām*) to God is for Muslims the model that they seek to imitate. God says in the Holy Qur'an:

> *Verily in the messenger of God ye have a goodly example for him who hopeth for God and the Last Day, and remembereth God much.* (*Al-Ahzab*, 33:21)

The totality of this love excludes worldliness and egotism, and is itself beautiful and loveable to Muslims. Love of God is itself loveable to Muslims. God says in the Holy Qur'an:

> *And know that the messenger of God is among you. If he were to obey you in many matters, ye would surely fall into misfortune; but God hath made the faith loveable to you and hath beautified it in your hearts, and hath made disbelief and lewdness and rebellion hateful unto you. Such are they who are the rightly guided.* (*Al-Hujurat*, 49:7)

[12] This 'particular love' is in addition to God's universal Mercy *which embraceth all things* (*Al-A'raf*, 7:156); but God knows best.

the devotional attitudes it demands, namely, loving and being devoted to God with all one's heart, all one's soul, all one's mind, all one's will or strength, and all one's sentiment. Hence the Prophet Muhammad (*'alayhi 'l-salāt^u wa 'l-salām*) commended this remembrance by saying:

> *He who says: 'There is no god but God, He Alone, He hath no associate, His is the sovereignty and His is the praise and He hath power over all things' one hundred times in a day, it is for them equal to setting ten slaves free, and one hundred good deeds are written for them and one hundred bad deeds are effaced, and it is for them a protection from the devil for that day until the evening. And none offers anything better than that, save one who does more than that.*[13]

[13] *Sahih Al-Bukhari, Kitab Bad' al-Khalq, Bab Sifat Iblis wa Junudihi*; *Hadith* no. 3329.

Other Versions of the Blessed Saying

This blessed saying of the Prophet Muhammad's (*'alayhi 'l-salāt^u wa 'l-salām*) is found in dozens of *hadith* (sayings of the Prophet Muhammad (*'alayhi 'l-salāt^u wa 'l-salām*)) in differing contexts in slightly varying versions.

The one we have quoted throughout in the text (*There is no god but God, He alone. He hath no associate. His is the sovereignty, and His is the praise, and He hath power over all things*) is in fact the shortest version. It is to be found in *Sahih al-Bukhari*: *Kitab al-Adhan* (no. 852); *Kitab al-Tahajjud* (no. 1163); *Kitab al-'Umrah* (no. 1825); *Kitab Bad' al-Khalq* (no. 3329); *Kitab al-Da'awat* (nos. 6404, 6458, 6477); *Kitab al-Riqaq* (no. 6551); *Kitab al-I'tisam bi'l-Kitab* (no. 7378); in *Sahih Muslim*: *Kitab al-Masajid* (nos. 1366, 1368, 1370, 1371, 1380); *Kitab al-Hajj* (nos. 3009, 3343); *Kitab al-Dhikr wa'l-Du'a'* (nos. 7018, 7020, 7082, 7084); in *Sunan Abu Dawud*: *Kitab al-Witr* (nos. 1506, 1507, 1508); *Kitab al-Jihad* (no. 2772); *Kitab al-Kharaj* (no. 2989); *Kitab al-Adab* (nos. 5062, 5073, 5079); in *Sunan al-Tirmidhi*: *Kitab al-Hajj* (no. 965); *Kitab al-Da'awat* (nos. 3718, 3743, 3984); in *Sunan al-Nasa'i*: *Kitab al-Sahw* (nos. 1347, 1348, 1349, 1350, 1351); *Kitab Manasik al-Hajj* (nos. 2985, 2997); *Kitab al-Iman wa'l-Nudhur* (no. 3793); in *Sunan Ibn Majah*: *Kitab al-Adab* (no. 3930); *Kitab al-Du'a'* (nos. 4000, 4011); and in *Muwatta' Malik*: *Kitab al-Qur'an* (nos. 492, 494); *Kitab al-Hajj* (no. 831).

A longer version including the words *yuhyi wa yumit*—(*There is no god but God, He alone. He hath no associate. His is the sovereignty, and His is the praise. He giveth life, and He giveth death, and He hath power over all things.*)—is to be found in *Sunan Abu Dawud*: *Kitab al-Manasik* (no. 1907); in *Sunan al-Tirmidhi*: *Kitab al-Salah* (no. 300); *Kitab al-Da'awat* (nos. 3804, 3811, 3877, 3901); and in *Sunan al-Nasa'i*: *Kitab Manasik al-Hajj* (nos. 2974, 2987, 2998); *Sunan Ibn Majah*: *Kitab al-Manasik* (no. 3190).

Another longer version including the words *bi yadihi al-khayr*—(*There is no god but God, He alone. He hath no associate. His is the sovereignty, and His is the praise. In His Hand is the good, and He hath power over all things.*)—is to be found in *Sunan Ibn Majah*: *Kitab al-Adab* (no. 3931); *Kitab al-Du'a'* (no. 3994).

The longest version, which includes the words *yuhyi wa yumit wa Huwa Hayyun la yamut bi yadihi al-khayr*—(*There is no god but God, He alone. He hath no associate. His is the sovereignty, and His is the praise. He giveth life, and He*

In other words, the blessed remembrance, *There is no god but God, He Alone, He hath no associate, His is the sovereignty and His is the praise and He hath power over all things*, not only requires and implies that Muslims must be totally devoted to God and love Him with their whole hearts and their whole souls and all that is in them, but provides a way, like its beginning (the testimony of faith)—through its frequent repetition[14]—for them to realize this love with everything they are.

giveth death. He is the Living, who dieth not. In His Hand is the good, and He hath power over all things.)—is to be found in *Sunan al-Tirmidhi*: *Kitab al-Da'awat* (no. 3756) and in *Sunan Ibn Majah*: *Kitab al-Tijarat* (no. 2320), with the difference that this latter *hadith* reads: *bi yadihi al-khayr kuluhu* (in His Hand is *all* good).

It is important to note, however, that the Prophet Muhammad (*'alayhi 'l-salāt[u] wa'l-salām*) only described the first (shortest) version as: *the best that I have said—myself, and the prophets that came before me*, and only of that version did the Prophet say: *And none comes with anything better than that, save one who does more than that.*

(These citations refer to the numbering system of *The Sunna Project's Encyclopaedia of Hadith* (*Jam' Jawami' al-Ahadith wa'l-Asanid*), prepared in cooperation with the scholars of al-Azhar, which includes *Sahih al-Bukhari, Sahih Muslim, Sunan Abu Dawud, Sunan al-Tirmidhi, Sunan al-Nasa'i, Sunan Ibn Majah*, and *Muwatta' Malik*.)

[14] *Frequent Remembrance of God in the Holy Qur'an*:
The Holy Qur'an is full of injunctions to invoke or remember God frequently:

> *Remember the name of thy Lord at morn and evening.* (*Al-Insan*, 76:25)
>
> *So remember God, standing, sitting and [lying] down on your sides* (*Al-Nisa*, 4:103).
>
> *And do thou (O Muhammad) remember thy Lord within thyself humbly and with awe, below thy breath, at morn and evening. And be not thou of the neglectful* (*Al-'Araf*, 7:205).
>
> ... *Remember thy Lord much, and praise (Him) in the early hours of night and morning* (*Aal 'Imran*, 3:41).
>
> *O ye who believe! Remember God with much remembrance. / And glorify Him early and late* (*Al-Ahzab*, 33:41-42).
>
> (See also: 2:198-200; 2:203; 2:238-239; 3:190-191; 6:91; 7:55; 7:180; 8:45; 17:110; 22:27-41; 24:35-38; 26:227; 62:9-10; 87:1-17, et al.)

Similarly, the Holy Qur'an is full of verses that emphasize the paramount importance of the Remembrance of God (see: 2:151-7; 5:4; 6:118; 7:201; 8:2-4; 13:26-28; 14:24-27; 20:14; 20:33-34; 24:1; 29:45; 33:35; 35:10; 39:9; 50:37; 51:55-58; and 33:2; 39:22-23 and 73:8-9 as already quoted, et al.), and the dire consequences of not practising it (see: 2:114; 4:142; 7:179-180; 18:28; 18:100-101; 20:99-101; 20:124-127; 25:18; 25:29; 43:36; 53:29; 58:19; 63:9; 72:17 et al.; see also 107:4-6). Hence God ultimately says in the Holy Qur'an:

> *Has not the time arrived for the believers that their hearts in all humility should engage in the remembrance of God .... ?* (*Al-Hadid*, 57:16);
>
> .... *[S]lacken not in remembrance of Me* (*Taha*, 20:42),
>
> and: *Remember your Lord whenever you forget* (*Al-Kahf*,

God says in one of the very first revelations in the Holy Qur'an: *So invoke the Name of thy Lord and devote thyself to Him with a complete devotion* (*Al-Muzzammil*, 73:8).

Love of God as the *First and Greatest Commandment* in the Bible

The *Shema* in the Book of Deuteronomy (6:4-5), a centrepiece of the Old Testament and of Jewish liturgy, says: *Hear, O Israel: The LORD our God, the LORD is one! / You shall love the LORD your God with all your heart, and with all your soul, and with all your strength.*[15]

Likewise, in the New Testament, when Jesus Christ (*'alayhi'l-salām*), the Messiah, is asked about the Greatest Commandment, he answers:

> *But when the Pharisees heard that he had silenced the Sadducees, they gathered together. / Then one of them, a lawyer, asked Him a question, testing Him, and saying, / "Teacher, which is the great commandment in the law?" / Jesus said to him, "'You shall love the LORD your God with all your heart, with all your soul, and with all your mind.' / This is the first and greatest commandment. / And the second is like it: 'You shall love your neighbour as yourself.' / On these two commandments hang all the Law and the Prophets."* (Matthew 22:34-40)

And also:

> *Then one of the scribes came, and having heard them reasoning together, perceiving that he had answered them well, asked him, "Which is the first commandment of all?" / Jesus answered him, "The first of all the commandments is: 'Hear, O Israel, the LORD our God, the LORD is one. / And you shall love the LORD your God with all your heart, with all your soul, with all your mind, and with all your strength.' This is the first commandment. / And the second, like it, is this: 'You shall love your neighbour as yourself.' There is no other*

18:24).

[15] Herein all Biblical Scripture is taken from the New King James Version. Copyright © 1982 by Thomas Nelson, Inc. Used by permission. All rights reserved.

commandment greater than these." (Mark 12:28-31)

The commandment to love God fully is thus the *First and Greatest Commandment* of the Bible. Indeed, it is to be found in a number of other places throughout the Bible including: Deuteronomy 4:29, 10:12, 11:13 (also part of the *Shema*), 13:3, 26:16, 30:2, 30:6, 30:10; Joshua 22:5; Mark 12:32-33 and Luke 10:27-28.

However, in various places throughout the Bible, it occurs in slightly different forms and versions. For instance, in Matthew 22:37 (*You shall love the LORD your God with all your heart, with all your soul, and with all your mind)*, the Greek word for "heart" is *kardia*, the word for "soul" is *psyche*, and the word for "mind" is *dianoia*. In the version from Mark 12:30 (*And you shall love the LORD your God with all your heart, with all your soul, with all your mind, and with all your strength*) the word "strength" is added to the aforementioned three, translating the Greek word *ischus*.

The words of the lawyer in Luke 10:27 (which are confirmed by Jesus Christ (*'alayhi 'l-salām*) in Luke 10:28) contain the same four terms as Mark 12:30. The words of the scribe in Mark 12:32 (which are approved of by Jesus Christ (*'alayhi 'l-salām*) in Mark 12:34) contain the three terms *kardia* ("heart"), *dianoia* ("mind"), and *ischus* ("strength").

In the *Shema* of Deuteronomy 6:4-5 (*Hear, O Israel: The LORD our God, the LORD is one! / You shall love the LORD your God with all your heart, and with all your soul, and with all your strength*). In Hebrew the word for "heart" is *lev*, the word for "soul" is *nefesh*, and the word for "strength" is *me'od*.

In Joshua 22:5, the Israelites are commanded by Joshua (*'alayhi 'l-salām*) to love God and be devoted to Him as follows:

> *"But take careful heed to do the commandment and the law which Moses the servant of the LORD commanded you, to love the LORD your God, to walk in all His ways, to keep His commandments, to hold fast to Him, and to serve Him with all your heart and with all your soul."* (Joshua 22:5)

What all these versions thus have in common—despite the language differences between the Hebrew Old Testament, the original words of Jesus Christ (*'alayhi 'l-salām*) in Aramaic, and the actual transmitted Greek of the New Testament—is the command to love God fully with one's heart and soul and to be fully devoted to Him.

This is the First and Greatest Commandment for human beings.

In the light of what we have seen to be necessarily implied and evoked by the Prophet Muhammad's (*'alayhi 'l-salāt*[u] *wa 'l-salām*) blessed saying: '*The best that I have said—myself, and the prophets that came before me—is: 'There is no god but God, He Alone, He hath no associate, His is the sovereignty and His is the praise and He hath power over all things*',[16] we can now perhaps understand the words '*The best that I have said—myself, and the prophets that came before me*' as equating the blessed formula *'There is no god but God, He Alone, He hath no associate, His is the sovereignty and His is the praise and He hath power over all things*' precisely with the 'First and Greatest Commandment' to love God, with all one's heart and soul, as found in various places in the Bible. That is to say, in other words, that the Prophet Muhammad (*'alayhi 'l-salāt*[u] *wa 'l-salām*) was perhaps, through inspiration, restating and alluding to the Bible's First Commandment. God knows best, but certainly we have seen their effective similarity in meaning. Moreover, we also do know (as can be seen in the endnotes), that both formulas have another remarkable parallel: the way they arise in a number of slightly differing versions and forms in different contexts, all of which, nevertheless, emphasize the primacy of total love and devotion to God.[17]

[16] *Sunan Al-Tirmithi, Kitab Al-Da'wat, Bab al-Du'a fi Yawm 'Arafah, Hadith* no. 3934. Op. cit.

[17] *In the Best Stature*:
Christianity and Islam have comparable conceptions of man being created in the best stature and from God's own breath. The Book of Genesis says:

> (Genesis, 1:27) *So God created man in His own image; in the image of God He created him; male and female He created them.*
> And:
> (Genesis, 2:7) *And the LORD God formed man of the dust of the ground, and breathed into his nostrils the breath of life; and man became a living being.*

And the Prophet Muhammad (*'alayhi 'l-salāt*[u] *wa 'l-salām*) said: *Verily God created Adam in His own image*. (*Sahih Al-Bukhari, Kitab Al-Isti'than*, 1; *Sahih Muslim, Kitab Al-Birr* 115; *Musnad Ibn Hanbal*, 2: 244, 251, 315, 323 etc. et al.)

> *And We created you, then fashioned you, then told the angels: Fall ye prostrate before Adam! And they fell prostrate, all save Iblis, who was not of those who make prostration.* (*Al-A'raf*, 7:11)
>
> *By the fig and the olive / By Mount Sinai, / And by this land made safe / Surely We created man of the best stature / Then*

(II) Love of the Neighbour

Love of the Neighbour in Islam

There are numerous injunctions in Islam about the necessity and paramount importance of love for—and mercy towards—the neighbour. Love of the neighbour is an essential and integral part of faith in God and love of God because in Islam without love of the neighbour there is no true faith in God and no righteousness. The Prophet Muhammad (*'alayhi 'l-salāt[u] wa 'l-salām*) said: "*None of you*

We reduced him to the lowest of the low, / Save those who believe and do good works, and theirs is a reward unfailing. / So who henceforth will give the lie to the about the judgment? / Is not God the wisest of all judges? (*Al-Tin*, 95:1-8)
God it is Who appointed for you the earth for a dwelling-place and the sky for a canopy, and fashioned you and perfected your shapes, and hath provided you with good things. Such is God, your Lord. Then blessed be God, the Lord of the Worlds! (*Al-Ghafir*, 40:64)

Nay, but those who do wrong follow their own lusts without knowledge. Who is able to guide him whom God hath sent astray? For such there are no helpers. / So set thy purpose (O Muhammad) for religion as a man by nature upright—tthe nature (framed) of God, in which He hath created man. There is no altering (the laws of) God's creation. That is the right religion, but most men know not—/ (*Al-Rum*, 30:29-30)

And when I have fashioned him and breathed into him of My Spirit, then fall down before him prostrate, (*Sad*, 38:72)

And when thy Lord said unto the angels: Lo! I am about to place a viceroy in the earth, they said: Wilt thou place therein one who will do harm therein and will shed blood, while we, we hymn Thy praise and sanctify Thee ? He said: Surely I know that which ye know not. / And He taught Adam all the names, then showed them to the angels, saying: Inform Me of the names of these, if ye are truthful ./ They said: Be glorified! We have no knowledge saving that which Thou hast taught us. Lo! Thou, only Thou, art the Knower, the Wise. / He said: O Adam! Inform them of their names, and when he had informed them of their names, He said: Did I not tell you that I know the secret of the heavens and the earth ? And I know that which ye disclose and which ye hide. / And when We said unto the angels: Prostrate yourselves before Adam, they fell prostrate, all save Iblis. He demurred through pride, and so became a disbeliever... / And We said: O Adam! Dwell thou and thy wife in the Garden, and eat ye freely (of the fruits) thereof where ye will; but come not nigh this tree lest ye become wrong-doers. (*Al-Baqarah*, 2:30-35) *has faith until you love for your brother what you love for yourself.*"[18] And: "*None of you has faith until you love for your neighbour what you love for yourself.*"[19]

However, empathy and sympathy for the neighbour—and even formal prayers— are not enough. They must be accompanied by generosity and self-sacrifice. God says in the Holy Qur'an:

> *It is not righteousness that ye turn your faces*[20] *to the East and the West; but righteous is he who believeth in God and the Last Day and the angels and the Scripture and the prophets; and giveth wealth, for love of Him, to kinsfolk and to orphans and the needy and the wayfarer and to those who ask, and to set slaves free; and observeth proper worship and payeth the poor-due. And those who keep their treaty when they make one, and the patient in tribulation and adversity and time of stress. Such are they who are sincere. Such are the pious.* (*Al-Baqarah*, 2:177)

And also:

> *Ye will not attain unto righteousness until ye expend of that which ye love. And whatsoever ye expend, God is Aware thereof.* (*Aal 'Imran*, 3:92)

Without giving the neighbour what we ourselves love, we do not truly love God or the neighbour.

Love of the Neighbour in the Bible

We have already cited the words of the Messiah, Jesus Christ (*'alayhi'l-salām*), about the paramount importance, second only to the love of God, of the love of the neighbour:

> *This is the first and greatest commandment. / And the second is like it: 'You shall love your neighbour as yourself.' / On these two commandments hang all the Law and the Prophets.* (Matthew 22:38-40)

[18] *Sahih Al-Bukhari, Kitab al-Iman, Hadith* no.13.

[19] *Sahih Muslim, Kitab al-Iman, 67-1, Hadith* no.45.

[20] The classical commentators on the Holy Qur'an (see: *Tafsir Ibn Kathir, Tafsir Al-Jalalayn*) generally agree that this is a reference to (the last movements of) the Muslim prayer.

And:

> *And the second, like it, is this: 'You shall love your neighbour as yourself.' There is no other commandment greater than these."* (Mark 12:31)

It remains only to be noted that this commandment is also to be found in the Old Testament:

> *You shall not hate your brother in your heart. You shall surely rebuke your neighbour, and not bear sin because of him. / You shall not take vengeance, nor bear any grudge against the children of your people, but you shall love your neighbour as yourself: I am the LORD.* (Leviticus 19:17-18)

Thus the Second Commandment, like the First Commandment, demands generosity and self-sacrifice, and *On these two commandments hang all the Law and the Prophets.*

(III) *Come to a Common Word Between Us and You*

A Common Word

Whilst Islam and Christianity are obviously different religions—and whilst there is no minimising some of their formal differences—it is clear that the *Two Greatest Commandments* are an area of common ground and a link between the Qur'an, the Torah and the New Testament. What prefaces the Two Commandments in the Torah and the New Testament, and what they arise out of, is the Unity of God—that there is only one God. For the *Shema* in the Torah, starts: (Deuteronomy 6:4) *Hear, O Israel: The LORD our God, the LORD is one!* Likewise, Jesus (*'alayhi 'l-salām*) said: (Mark 12:29) "*The first of all the commandments is: 'Hear, O Israel, the LORD our God, the LORD is one"*." Likewise, God says in the Holy Qur'an: *Say: He, God, is One. / God, the Self-Sufficient Besought of all.* (*Al-Ikhlas*, 112:1-2). Thus the Unity of God, love of Him, and love of the neighbour form a common ground upon which Islam and Christianity (and Judaism) are founded.

This could not be otherwise since Jesus (*'alayhi 'l-salām*) said: (Matthew 22:40) "*On these two commandments hang all the Law and the Prophets.*" Moreover, God confirms in the Holy Qur'an that the

Prophet Muhammad (*'alayhi'l-salāt[u] wa'l-salām*) brought nothing fundamentally or essentially new: *Naught is said to thee (Muhammad) but what already was said to the messengers before thee* (*Fussilat* 41:43). And: *Say (Muhammad): I am no new thing among the messengers (of God), nor know I what will be done with me or with you. I do but follow that which is Revealed to me, and I am but a plain warner* (*Al-Ahqaf*, 46:9). Thus also God in the Holy Qur'an confirms that the same eternal truths of the Unity of God, of the necessity for total love and devotion to God (and thus shunning false gods), and of the necessity for love of fellow human beings (and thus justice), underlie all true religion:

> *And verily We have raised in every nation a messenger, (proclaiming): Worship God and shun false gods. Then some of them (there were) whom God guided, and some of them (there were) upon whom error had just hold. Do but travel in the land and see the nature of the consequence for the deniers!* (*Al-Nahl*, 16:36)
>
> *We verily sent Our messengers with clear proofs, and revealed with them the Scripture and the Balance, that mankind may stand forth in justice....* (*Al-Hadid*, 57:25)

Come to a Common Word!

In the Holy Qur'an, God Most High tells Muslims to issue the following call to Christians (and Jews—the *People of the Scripture*):

> *Say: O People of the Scripture! Come to a common word between us and you: that we shall worship none but God, and that we shall ascribe no partner unto Him, and that none of us shall take others for lords beside God. And if they turn away, then say: Bear witness that we are they who have surrendered (unto Him).* (*Aal 'Imran* 3:64)

Clearly, the blessed words: *we shall ascribe no partner unto Him* relate to the Unity of God. Clearly also, worshipping *none but God*, relates to being totally devoted to God and hence to the *First and Greatest Commandment*. According to one of the oldest and most authoritative commentaries (*tafsir*) on the Holy Qur'an—the *Jami' Al-Bayan fi Ta'wil Al-Qur'an* of Abu Ja'far Muhammad bin Jarir Al-Tabari (d. 310 A.H. / 923 C.E.)—*that none of us shall take others for lords beside God*, means 'that none of us should obey in disobedience to what God has commanded, nor glorify them by prostrating to them in the same way as they prostrate to God'. In other words, that Muslims, Christians and Jews should be free to each follow what God commanded them, and not have 'to prostrate before kings and the like'[21]; for God says elsewhere in the Holy Qur'an: *Let there be no compulsion in religion....* (*Al-Baqarah*, 2:256). This clearly relates to the Second Commandment and to love of the neighbour of which justice[22] and freedom of religion are a crucial part. God says in the Holy Qur'an:

> *God forbiddeth you not those who warred not against you on account of religion and drove you not out from your homes, that ye should show them kindness and deal justly with them. Lo! God loveth the just dealers.* (*Al-Mumtahinah*, 60:8)

We thus as Muslims invite Christians to remember Jesus's (*'alayhi 'l-salām*) words in the Gospel (Mark 12:29-31):

> *... the LORD our God, the LORD is one. / And you shall love the LORD your God with all your heart, with all your soul, with all your mind, and with all your strength. 'This is the first commandment. / And the second, like it, is this: 'You shall love your neighbour as yourself.' There is no other commandment greater than these.*

As Muslims, we say to Christians that we are not against them and that Islam is not against them—so long as they do not wage war against Muslims on account of their religion, oppress them and drive them out of their homes, (in accordance with the verse of the Holy Qur'an [*Al-Mumtahinah*, 60:8] quoted above). Moreover, God says in the Holy Qur'an:

> *They are not all alike. Of the People of the Scripture there is a staunch community who recite the revelations of God in the night season, falling prostrate (before Him). / They believe in God and the Last Day, and enjoin right conduct and forbid*

[21] Abu Ja'far Muhammad Bin Jarir Al-Tabari, *Jami' al-Bayan fi Ta'wil al-Qur'an*, (*Dar al-Kutub al-'Ilmiyyah*, Beirut, Lebanon, 1st ed, 1992/1412,) *tafsir* of *Aal-'Imran*, 3:64; Volume 3, pp. 299-302.

[22] According to grammarians cited by Tabari (op cit.) the word 'common' (*sawa'*) in 'a common word between us' also means 'just', 'fair' (*adl*).

indecency, and vie one with another in good works. These are of the righteous. / And whatever good they do, nothing will be rejected of them. God is Aware of those who ward off (evil). (*Aal-'Imran*, 3:113-115)

Is Christianity necessarily against Muslims? In the Gospel Jesus Christ (*'alayhi 'l-salām*) says:

He who is not with me is against me, and he who does not gather with me scatters abroad. (Matthew 12:30) *For he who is not against us is on our side.* (Mark 9:40) *... for he who is not against us is on our side.* (Luke 9:50)

According to the *Blessed Theophylact's*[23] *Explanation of the New Testament*, these statements are not contradictions because the first statement (in the actual Greek text of the New Testament) refers to demons, whereas the second and third statements refer to people who recognised Jesus (*'alayhi 'l-salām*), but were not Christians. Muslims recognize Jesus Christ (*'alayhi 'l-salām*) as the Messiah, not in the same way Christians do (but Christians themselves anyway have never all agreed with each other on Jesus Christ's (*'alayhi 'l-salām*) nature), but in the following way: .... *the Messiah Jesus son of Mary is a Messenger of God and His Word which he cast unto Mary and a Spirit from Him....* (*Al-Nisa'*, 4:171). We therefore invite Christians to consider Muslims *not against* and thus *with them*, in accordance with Jesus Christ's (*'alayhi 'l-salām*) words here.

Finally, as Muslims, and in obedience to the Holy Qur'an, we ask Christians to come together with us on the common essentials of our two religions ... *that we shall worship none but God, and that we shall ascribe no partner unto Him, and that none of us shall take others for lords beside God ... (Aal 'Imran*, 3:64).

Let this common ground be the basis of all future interfaith dialogue between us, for our common ground is that on which hangs *all the Law and the Prophets* (Matthew 22:40). God says in the Holy Qur'an:

Say (O Muslims): We believe in God and that which is revealed unto us and that which was revealed unto Abraham,

[23] The Blessed Theophylact (1055-1108 C.E.) was the Orthodox Archbishop of Ochrid and Bulgaria (1090-1108 C.E.). His native language was the Greek of the New Testament. His *Commentary* is currently available in English from Chrysostom Press.

and Ishmael, and Isaac, and Jacob, and the tribes, and that which Moses and Jesus received, and that which the prophets received from their Lord. We make no distinction between any of them, and unto Him we have surrendered. / And if they believe in the like of that which ye believe, then are they rightly guided. But if they turn away, then are they in schism, and God will suffice thee against them. He is the Hearer, the Knower. (*Al-Baqarah*, 2:136-137)

Between Us and You

Finding common ground between Muslims and Christians is not simply a matter for polite ecumenical dialogue between selected religious leaders. Christianity and Islam are the largest and second largest religions in the world and in history. Christians and Muslims reportedly make up over a third and over a fifth of humanity respectively. Together they make up more than 55% of the world's population, making the relationship between these two religious communities the most important factor in contributing to meaningful peace around the world. If Muslims and Christians are not at peace, the world cannot be at peace. With the terrible weaponry of the modern world; with Muslims and Christians intertwined everywhere as never before, no side can unilaterally win a conflict between more than half of the world's inhabitants. Thus our common future is at stake. The very survival of the world itself is perhaps at stake.

And to those who nevertheless relish conflict and destruction for their own sake or reckon that ultimately they stand to gain through them, we say that our very eternal souls are all also at stake if we fail to sincerely make every effort to make peace and come together in harmony. God says in the Holy Qur'an: *Lo! God enjoineth justice and kindness, and giving to kinsfolk, and forbiddeth lewdness and abomination and wickedness. He exhorteth you in order that ye may take heed* (*Al Nahl*, 16:90). Jesus Christ (*'alayhi'l-salām*) said: *Blessed are the peacemakers ….*(Matthew 5:9), and also: *For what profit is it to a man if he gains the whole world and loses his soul?* (Matthew 16:26).

So let our differences not cause hatred and strife between us. Let us vie with each other only in righteousness and good works. Let us respect each other, be fair, just and kind to another and live in sincere peace, harmony and mutual goodwill. God says in the Holy Qur'an:

> *And unto thee have We revealed the Scripture with the truth, confirming whatever Scripture was before it, and a watcher over it. So judge between them by that which God hath revealed, and follow not their desires away from the truth which hath come unto thee. For each We have appointed a law and a way. Had God willed He could have made you one community. But that He may try you by that which He hath given you (He hath made you as ye are). So vie one with another in good works. Unto God ye will all return, and He will then inform you of that wherein ye differ.* (*Al-Ma'idah*, 5:48)

Wal-Salaamu 'Alaykum,
Pax Vobiscum.

A Common Word Between Us and You

A Response by David Ford

This historic statement gives the right keynote for relations between Muslims and Christians in the 21st century. It is what we have been missing since 9/11/2001. The most impressive list of signatories from all the main Muslim traditions and countries have made a clear and powerful proclamation of love for God and for all neighbours. The message is rich and deep, and it goes to the heart of Muslim faith as expressed in the Quran. It also goes to the heart of the teaching of Jesus in the New Testament.

There are three main reasons why this is so important.

First, it is unprecedented in bringing together so many of the leading religious authorities and scholars of Islam and uniting them in a positive, substantial affirmation. This is an astonishing achievement of solidarity, one that can be built on in the future.

Second, it is addressed to Christians in the form of a friendly word, it engages respectfully and carefully with the Christian scriptures, and it finds common ground in what Jesus himself said is central: love of God and love of neighbour. I like its modesty—it does not claim to be the final word but to be "a common word," one that Muslims and Christians (and, I would also add, Jews and many others) can share with integrity. This is shared ground, mutual ground, where there is the possibility of working further on issues that unite and divide us. This common word does not pretend that there are no differences between Muslims and Christians (for example, on the Christian teaching *about* Jesus rather than the teaching *of* Jesus). It takes a vital step forward, and wisely does this by concentrating mainly on each tradition's scriptures, those core texts that are so often misused but which, in my experience, also have the resources for enabling deeper mutual understanding and trust.

Third, it opens a way forward that is more hopeful for the world than most others at present in the public sphere. Its combination of

Islamic solidarity around core teaching together with friendly address to Christians should be seen as setting a direction for the twenty-first century. It challenges Muslims and Christians to live up to their own teachings and seek political and educational as well as personal ways to do this for the sake of the common good. It invites them to go deeper into their own faith at the same time as going deeper into each other's. It cries out to be followed through by many initiatives in the same spirit. These should be among Muslims, among Christians, between Muslims and Christians, and between them and those of other faiths and no faith. They should be in many spheres of life and at all levels—local, regional and global. It is deeply encouraging that the Royal Academy of Jordan has had the courage, imagination and practical capacity to achieve this. Now the Royal Academy needs to be joined by many others in following this through.

An obvious question is: but will this have any impact on the violent extremism that afflicts the world? I do not think that problem has a simple one-off solution. But any long-term solution will have to include four elements:

- Muslim solidarity around an understanding of their faith that clearly excludes violent, uncompassionate acts, programmes and language;
- better Christian understanding of Islam;
- deeper engagement between Muslims and Christians that makes use of the resources at the heart of their faith, such as their scriptures;
- a concern for the nourishing of the whole human family and the whole planet.

I find all four in "A Common Word." If sufficient people and groups heed this statement and act on it then the atmosphere will be changed into one in which violent extremists cannot flourish.

I think that many people have longed for a statement like this. Its significance is not that it offers anything novel but that it selects so wisely from the riches of both scriptures and opens them up in a way that is highly relevant to the present situation. I found myself deeply moved by its vision of what it calls "the all-embracing, constant and active love of God" and "the necessity and paramount importance of love for—and mercy towards—the neighbour," and by its concern not only for that half of the world's population who are Muslim or Christian but also for every single other person and the whole of creation.

A Common Word for the Common Good

To
the Muslim Religious Leaders and Scholars
who have signed
A Common Word Between Us and You
and to Muslim brothers and sisters everywhere

From the Archbishop of Canterbury
The Very Rev. Dr. Rowan Williams

Grace, Mercy and Peace be with you

Preface

Dear Friends:

We are deeply appreciative of the initiative you have taken and welcome *A Common Word Between Us and You* as a significant development in relations between Christians and Muslims. In your letter you have addressed 27 Christian leaders and "leaders of Christian Churches everywhere" and many of those addressed have already responded or set in motion processes through which responses will in due course be made. Having listened carefully to Christian colleagues from the widest possible range of backgrounds, most significantly at a Consultation of Church representatives and Christian scholars in June 2008, I am pleased to offer this response to your letter, with their support and encouragement.

We recognise that your letter brings together Muslim leaders from many traditions of Islam to address Christian leaders representative of the diverse traditions within Christianity. We find in it a hospitable and friendly spirit, expressed in its focus on love of God and love of neighbour—a focus which draws together the languages of Christianity and Islam, and of Judaism also. Your letter could hardly be more timely, given the growing awareness that peace throughout the world is deeply entwined with the ability of all people of faith everywhere to live in peace, justice, mutual respect and love. Our belief is that only through a commitment to that transcendent perspective to which your letter points, and to which we also look, shall we find the resources for radical, transforming, non-violent engagement with the deepest needs of our world and our common humanity.

In your invitation to "come to a common word" we find a helpful generosity of intention. Some have read the invitation as an insistence that we should be able immediately to affirm an agreed and shared understanding of God. But such an affirmation would not be honest to either of our traditions. It would fail to acknowledge the reality of the differences that exist and that have been the cause of deep and—at times in the past—even violent division. We read your letter as expressing a more modest but ultimately a more realistically hopeful recognition that the ways in which we as Christians and Muslims speak about God and humanity are not simply mutually unintelligible systems. We interpret your invitation as saying 'let us find a way of recognising that on some matters we are speaking enough of a common language for us to be able to pursue both exploratory dialogue and peaceful co-operation with integrity and without compromising fundamental beliefs.'

We find this recognition in what is, for us, one of the key paragraphs of your letter:

> "In the light of what we have seen to be necessarily implied and evoked by the Prophet Muhammad's (pbuh) blessed saying: *'The best that I have said—myself, and the prophets that came before me—is: "there is no god but God, He Alone, He hath no associate, His is the sovereignty and His is the praise and He hath power over all things"'*, we can now perhaps understand the words *'The best that I have said—myself, and the prophets that came before me'* as equating the blessed formula *'there is no god but God, He Alone, He hath no associate, His is the sovereignty and His is the praise and He hath power over all things'* precisely with the 'First and Greatest Commandment' to love God, with all one's heart and soul, as found in various places in the Bible. That is to say, in other words, that the Prophet Muhammad (pbuh) was perhaps, through inspiration, restating and alluding to the

> Bible's First Commandment. God knows best, but certainly we have seen their effective similarity in meaning. Moreover, we also do know (as can be seen in the endnotes), that both formulas have another remarkable parallel: the way they arise in a number of slightly differing versions and forms in different contexts, all of which, nevertheless, emphasize the primacy of total love and devotion to God."

The double use of 'perhaps' in that passage allows for openness, exploration and debate—made possible because certain aspects of the ways in which we structure our talk about God in our respective traditions are intelligible one to the other. We read it as an invitation to further discussion within the Christian family and within the Muslim family as well as between Muslims and Christians, since it invites all of us to think afresh about the foundations of our convictions. There are many things between us that offer the promise of deeper insight through future discussion. Thus for us your letter makes a highly significant contribution to the divinely initiated journey into which we are called, the journey in which Christians and Muslims alike are taken further into mutual understanding and appreciation. The confession that "God knows best" reminds us of the limits of our understanding and knowledge.

In the light of this letter, what are the next steps for us? We draw from *A Common Word Between Us and You* five areas which might be fruitfully followed through.

First, its focus on the love and praise of God, stressing how we must trust absolutely in God and give him the devotion of our whole being—heart, mind and will—underlines a shared commitment: the fixed intention to relate all reality and all behaviour intelligently, faithfully and practically to the God who deals with us in love, compassion, justice and peace. One of the areas we can usefully discuss together is the diverse ways in which we understand the love of God as an absolutely free gift to his creation. There are bound to be differences as well as similarities in the ways we understand and express God's love for us and how we seek to practise love for God and neighbour in return, and in what follows we consider how these might be explored in a spirit of honest and co-operative attention.

Second, its commitment to a love of neighbour that is rooted in the love of God (and which, for Christians, is part of our response to the love of God for us) suggests that we share a clear passion for the common good of all humanity and all creation. In what follows we shall seek to identify some practical implications for our future relations both with each other and with the rest of the world.

Third, the concern to ground what we say in the Scriptures of our traditions shows a desire to meet each other not 'at the margins' of our historic identities but speaking from what is central and authoritative for us Here, however, it is especially important to acknowledge that the Qur'an's role in Islam is not the same as that of the Bible in Christianity; Christians understand the primary location of God's revealing Word to be the history of God's people and above all the history of Jesus Christ, whom we acknowledge as the Word made flesh, to which the Bible is the authoritative and irreplaceable witness. For the Muslim, as we understand it, the Word is supremely communicated in what Mohammed is commanded to recite. But for both faiths, scripture provides the basic tools for speaking of God and it is in attending to how we use our holy texts that we often discover most truly the nature of each other's faith.[1] In what follows we shall suggest how studying our scriptures together might continue to provide a fruitful element of our engagements with each other in the process of "building a home together", to pick up an image popularised by Rabbi Jonathan Sacks in a recent book.[2]

Fourth, and growing out of this last point, the letter encourages us to relate to each other from the heart of our lives of faith before God. However much or little 'common ground' we initially sense between us, it is possible to engage with each other without anxiety if we truly begin from the heart of what we believe we have received from God; possible to speak together, respecting and discussing differences rather than imprisoning ourselves in mutual fear and suspicion.

[1] As the staff of the Pontifical Institute for Arabic and Islamic Studies wrote in their appreciation of your letter: "We are pleased to see that the biblical and Gospel quotations used in this document come from the sources and that explanations given are on occasion based on the original languages: Hebrew, Aramaic and Greek. This is evidence of deep respect and genuine attentiveness to others, while at the same time of a true scientific spirit."(issued by Pontificio Istituto di Studi Arabi e d'Islamistica [PISAI], Rome, 25th October 2007)

[2] Jonathan Sacks, *The Home We Build Together: Recreating Society* (London: Continuum, 2007)

Finally, we acknowledge gratefully your recognition that the differences between Christians and Muslims are real and serious and that you do not claim to address all the issues. Yet in offering this focus on love of God and neighbour, you identify what could be the centre of a sense of shared calling and shared responsibility—an awareness of what God calls for from all his human creatures to whom he has given special responsibility in creation. In our response, it is this search for a common awareness of responsibility before God that we shall seek to hold before us as a vision worthy of our best efforts.

This response therefore looks in several directions. It seeks to encourage more reflection within the Christian community, as well as to promote honest encounter between Christian and Muslim believers; and it asks about the possible foundations for shared work in the world and a shared challenge to all those things which obscure God's purpose for humanity.

The One God Who is Love

At the origins of the history of God's people, as Jewish and Christian Scripture record it, is the command given to Moses to communicate to the people—the *Shema,* as it has long been known, from its opening word in Hebrew:

> **Hear, O Israel: The LORD our God, the LORD is one!**
>
> **You shall love the LORD your God with all your heart, and with all your soul, and with all your strength.** [3]
> (Deuteronomy 6:4-5)[4]

Such an imperative, as your letter makes clear, is of central authority for Muslims too.

Hear, O Israel: The LORD our God, the LORD is one!: The *tawhid* principle[5] is held out in your letter as one of the bases for agreement. In addition to the passages you quote to demonstrate *tawhid,* we read in the Qur'an:

[3] Taken from the *English Standard Version* of the Bible.

[4] Unless otherwise stated, quotations from the Bible are taken from the *New Revised Standard Version* (copyright 1989 by the Division of Christian Education of the National Council of Churches of Christ in the USA).

[5] *Tawhid:* that God is one, monotheism. *shirk:* the association of God with other beings who are not divine, whether other 'gods', saints, mediators of various kinds.

> *God: there is no god but Him, the Ever Living, the Ever Watchful.*[6] (al-Baqara 2:255)[7]
>
> *He is God the One, God the eternal. He fathered no one nor was he fathered.*
> *No one is comparable to Him.* (al-Ikhlas 112:1-4)

This last text reminds the Christian that this great affirmation of the uniqueness of God is what has often caused Muslims to look with suspicion at the Christian doctrines of God. Christian belief about the Trinity—God as Father, Son and Holy Spirit—appears at once to compromise the belief that God has no other being associated with him. How can we call God *al-Qayyum*, the Self-sufficient, if he is not alone? So we read in the Qur'an

> *The East and the West belong to God: wherever you turn, there is His Face.*
> *God is all pervading and all knowing. They have asserted, "God has a child."*
> *May He be exalted! No! Everything in the heavens and earth belongs to Him,*
> *everything devoutly obeys His will. He is the Originator of the heavens and the earth, and when He decrees something, He says only "Be," and it is.* (al-Baqara 2:115-117)

Muslims see the belief that God could have a son as suggesting that God is somehow limited as we are limited, bound to physical processes and needing the co-operation of others. How can such a God be truly free and sovereign—qualities both Christianity and Islam claim to affirm, for we know that God is able to bring the world into being by his word alone?

Here it is important to state unequivocally that the association of any other being with God is expressly rejected by the Christian theological tradition. Since the earliest Councils of the Church, Christian thinkers sought to clarify how, when we speak of the Father 'begetting' the Son, we must put out of our minds any suggestion that this is a physical thing, a process or event like the processes and events that happen in the world. They insisted that the name 'God' is not the

[6] *Al-Qayyum* can also be translated as "Self-subsistent" and "Self-sufficient".

[7] Unless otherwise stated all quotations from the Qur'an are taken from *A new translation* by M. A. S. Abdel Haleem (Oxford: OUP, 2005).

name of a person like a human person, a limited being with a father and mother and a place that they inhabit within the world. 'God' is the name of a kind of life, a 'nature' or essence—eternal and self-sufficient life, always active, needing nothing. But that life is lived, so Christians have always held, eternally and simultaneously as three interrelated agencies are made known to us in the history of God's revelation to the Hebrew people and in the life of Jesus and what flows from it. God is at once the source of divine life, the expression of that life and the active power that communicates that life. This takes us at once into consideration of the Trinitarian language used by Christians to speak of God. We recognise that this is difficult, sometimes offensive, to Muslims; but it is all the more important for the sake of open and careful dialogue that we try to clarify what we do and do not mean by it, and so trust that what follows will be read in this spirit.

In human language, in the light of what our Scripture says, we speak of "Father, Son and Holy Spirit", but we do not mean one God with two beings alongside him, or three gods of limited power. So there is indeed one God, the Living and Self-subsistent, associated with no other; but what God is and does is not different from the life which is eternally and simultaneously the threefold pattern of life: source and expression and sharing. Since God's life is always an intelligent, purposeful and loving life, it is possible to think of each of these dimensions of divine life as, in important ways, like a centre of mind and love, a person; but this does not mean that God 'contains' three different individuals, separate from each other as human individuals are.

Christians believe that in a mysterious manner we have a limited share in the characteristics of divine life.[8] Through the death and rising to life of Jesus, God takes away our evildoing and our guilt, he forgives us and sets us free. And our Scriptures go on to say[9] that he breathes new life into us, as he breathed life into Adam at the first, so that God's spirit is alive in us. The presence and action of the Holy

[8] **God is love. Whoever lives in love lives in God and God in him** (1John 4:16); see also 2Peter 1.4: **Thus** [God] **has given us, through these things, his precious and very great promises, so that through them you may escape from the corruption that is in the world because of lust, and may become participants in the divine nature.**

[9] As in Paul's First Letter to the Corinthians, 15.45-49 and the Letter to the Galatians, 4.6, for example.

Spirit is thus God in his action of sharing life with us.[10] As we become mature in our new life, our lives become closer and closer (so we pray and hope) to the central and perfect expression of divine life, the Word whom we encounter in Jesus—though we never become simply equal to him. And because Jesus prayed to the source of his life as 'Father',[11] we call the eternal and perfect expression of God's life not only the Word but also the 'Son'. We pray to the source of divine life in the way that Jesus taught us, and we say 'Father' to this divine reality. And in calling the eternal word the 'Son' of God, we remind ourselves that he is in no way different in nature from the Father: there is only one divine nature and reality.

Because God exists in this threefold pattern of interdependent action, the relationship between Father, Son and Holy Spirit is one in which there is always a 'giving place' to each other, each standing back so that the other may act. The only human language we have for this is *love*: the three dimensions of divine life relate to each other in self-sacrifice or self-giving. The doctrine of the Trinity is a way of explaining why we say that God *is* love, not only that he shows love.

When God acts towards us in compassion to liberate us from evil, to deal with the consequences of our rebellion against him and to make us able to call upon him with confidence, it is a natural (but not automatic) flowing outwards of his own everlasting action. The mutual self-giving love that is the very life of God is made real for our sake in the self-giving love of Jesus. And it is because of God's prior love for us that we are enabled and enjoined to love God.[12] Through our loving response, we can begin to comprehend something of God's nature and God's will for humankind:

> "**Whoever does not love does not know God, because God is love**" (1John 4:8).

[10] **God's love has been poured into our hearts through the Holy Spirit that has been given to us** (Romans 5:5).

[11] In Matthew 6:9-15 Jesus says: **"Pray then in this way: Our Father in heaven, hallowed be your name. [1]Your kingdom come. Your will be done, on earth as it is in heaven. [1]Give us this day our daily bread. [1]And forgive us our debts, as we also have forgiven our debtors. [1]And do not bring us to the time of trial, but rescue us from the evil one. [14]For if you forgive others their trespasses, your heavenly Father will also forgive you; [15]but if you do not forgive others, neither will your Father forgive your trespasses."**

[12] Something similar seems to be implied by the ordering of the loves in the Qur'anic verse 5:54 in which it is said that "*God will bring a new people: He will love them, and they will love Him.*"

So Christians go further than simply saying that God is a loving God or that love is one of his attributes among others. We say that God does not love simply because he *decides* to love. God is always, eternally, loving—the very nature and definition of God is love, and the full understanding of his unity is for Christians bound up with this.

Understanding the **"breadth and length and height and depth"** of the love of God[13] is a lifetime's journey; so it is not remotely possible to consider it with satisfactory thoroughness within the confines of this letter. However, it is necessary at this point to stress two qualities of God's love that are crucially important for the Christian: it is unconditional,[14] given gratuitously and without cause; and it is self-sacrificial.[15]

In the birth, life, death, resurrection and ascension of Jesus Christ, the loving nature of God is revealed. We see how Jesus, both in his ministry and in his acceptance of a sacrificial death at the hands of his enemies, offers a love that is given in advance of any human response; it is not a reward for goodness—rather it is what makes human goodness possible, as we change our lives in gratitude to God for his free gift. In the words of a well-known English hymn, it is "Love to the loveless shown, that they might lovely be".[16] And because of this, it is also a love that is vulnerable. God does not convert us and transform us by exercising his divine power alone. So infinite is that power, and so inseparable from love, that no defeat or suffering, even the terrible suffering of Jesus on the cross, can overcome God's purpose.

So, when we seek to live our lives in love of God and neighbour, we as Christians pray that we may be given strength to love God even when God does not seem to give us what we think we want or seems far off (a major theme in the writings of many Christian mystics, who often speak of those moments of our experience when God does not

[13] **I pray that you may have the power to comprehend, with all the saints, what is the breadth and length and height and depth, and to know the love of Christ that surpasses knowledge, so that you may be filled with all the fullness of God.** (Ephesians 3:18-19)

[14] One of the most influential and beloved New Testament texts illuminating the love of God is the parable of the Prodigal Son—sometimes called the parable of the Loving Father (Luke 15:11-32).

[15] **"For God so loved the world that he gave his one and only begotten Son, that whoever believes in him shall not perish but have eternal life"** (John 3:16).

[16] in "My song is love unknown" by Samuel Crossman (1664).

seem to love us as we should want to be loved); and we pray too for the strength to love those who do not seem to deserve our love, to love those who reject our love, to love those who have not yet made any move in love towards us.

We seek to show in our lives some of the characteristics of God's own love. We know that this may mean putting ourselves at risk; to love where we can see no possibility of love being returned is to be vulnerable, and we can only dare to do this in the power of God's Holy Spirit, creating in us some echo, some share, of Christ's own love. And in the light of all this, one area where dialogue between Christians and Muslims will surely be fruitful is in clarifying how far Muslims can in good conscience go in seeing the love of God powerfully at work in circumstances where the world sees only failure or suffering—but also, to anticipate the challenge that some Muslims might make in answer, how far the Christian tradition of accepting suffering on this basis may sometimes lead to a passive attitude to suffering and a failure to try and transform situations in the name of God's justice.

Thus, as Christians, we would say that our worship of God as threefold has never compromised the unity of God, which we affirm as wholeheartedly as Jews and Muslims. Indeed, by understanding God as a unity of love we see ourselves intensifying and enriching our belief in the unity of God. This indivisible unity is again expressed in the ancient theological formula, which we can trace back to the North African theologian Saint Augustine, *opera Trinitatis ad extra indivisa sunt*—all the actions of the Trinity outside itself are indivisible. So, although the Trinity has been a point of dispute with Jews and Muslims, and will no doubt continue to be so, we are encouraged that *A Common Word Between Us and You* does not simply assume that Christians believe in more than one god.[17] We are, therefore, encouraged in the

[17] We understand that this is the reading given to the Qur'anic verse al-Zumar 29:46 ("*our God and your God are one [and the same]*") and Aal 'Imran, 3:113-115, quoted in your letter. It is also our interpretation of the passage in your letter that reads: 'Clearly, the blessed words: *we shall ascribe no partner unto Him* relate to the Unity of God. Clearly also, worshipping *none but God*, relates to being totally devoted to God and hence to the *First and Greatest Commandment*. According to one of the oldest and most authoritative commentaries (*tafsir*) on the Holy Qur'an—the *Jami' Al-Bayan fi Ta'wil Al-Qur'an* of Abu Ja'far Muhammad bin Jarir Al-Tabari (d. 310 A.H. / 923 C.E.)—*that none of us shall take others for lords beside God*, means "that none of us should obey in disobedience to what God has commanded, nor glorify them by prostrating to them in the same way as

belief that what both our faiths say concerning the nature of God is not totally diverse—there are points of communication and overlap in the way we think about the divine nature that make our continued exploration of these issues worthwhile, despite the important issues around whether we can say that God is love in his very nature.

It was, therefore, appropriate that Cardinal Bertone, in his letter to Prince Ghazi bin Muhammad bin Talal welcoming *A Common Word Between Us and You* on behalf of Pope Benedict XVI, wrote:

> Without ignoring or downplaying our differences as Christians and Muslims, we can and therefore should look to what unites us, namely, belief in the one God, the provident Creator and universal Judge who at the end of time will deal with each person according to his or her actions. We are all called to commit ourselves totally to him and to obey his sacred will.[18]

To what extent do the Christian conviction of God as Love and the all-important Islamic conviction that God is "the Compassionate, the Merciful" *(al-Rahman al-Rahim)* represent common ground, and to what extent do differences need to be spelled out further? This is a very significant area for further work. But your letter—and many of the Christian responses to it—do make it clear that we have a basis on which we can explore such matters together in a spirit of genuine—and truly neighbourly!—love.

Responding to the Gift of Love

> **Beloved, let us love one another, because love is from God; everyone who loves is born of God and knows God. Whoever does not love does not know God, for God is love. God's love was revealed among us in this way: God sent his only Son into the world so that we might live through him. In this is love, not that we loved God but that he loved us and sent his Son to be the atoning sacrifice for our**

they prostrate to God". In other words, that Muslims, Christians and Jews should be free to each follow what God commanded them, and not have "to prostrate before kings and the like"; for God says elsewhere in the Holy Qur'an: *Let there be no compulsion in religion....* (*Al-Baqarah*, 2:256). This clearly relates to the Second Commandment and to love of the neighbour of which justice and freedom of religion are a crucial part.'

[18] Letter dated 19 November 2007.

> **sins. Beloved, since God loved us so much, we also ought to love one another. No one has ever seen God; if we love one another, God lives in us, and his love is perfected in us.** (1John 4:7-12)
>
> *God will bring a new people: He will love them, and they will love Him.* (al-Ma'ida 5:54).

What has been said so far is intended to highlight the way in which we as Christians see love as first and foremost a gift from God to us which makes possible for us a new level of relation with God and one another. By God's outpouring of love, we come to share in the kind of life that is characteristic of God's own eternal life. Our love of God appears as a response to God's prior love for us in its absolute gratuity and causelessness.

Thus to speak of our love for God is before all else to speak in words of praise and gratitude. And for both Jews and Christians, that language of praise has been shaped by and centred upon the Psalms of David:

> 1 **I will extol you, my God and King, and bless your name forever and ever.**
>
> 2 **Every day I will bless you, and praise your name forever and ever.**
>
> 3 **Great is the LORD, and greatly to be praised; his greatness is unsearchable.**
>
> ...
>
> 15 **The eyes of all look to you, and you give them their food in due season.**
>
> 16 **You open your hand, satisfying the desire of every living thing.**
>
> ...
>
> 21 **My mouth will speak the praise of the LORD, and all flesh will bless his holy name forever and ever.** (Psalm 145)

In words like these, we hear many resonances with the language of your letter, suggesting a similar kind of devotion expressed in words of love, praise and thanks. The language of the Psalms, like the language you have used, looks to a God of ultimate creative power who is loving and compassionate, generous, faithful and merciful, and upholds justice. In the Psalms, generation after generation has found inspiration and encouragement in the heights, depths and ordinariness of human life. Countless Christians and Jews use them daily. They show, in the words of your letter, how worshippers "must be grateful to God and trust Him with all their sentiments and emotions", and that "the call to be totally devoted and attached to God heart and soul, far from being a call for a mere emotion or for a mood, is in fact an injunction requiring all-embracing, constant and active love of God. It demands a love in which the innermost spiritual heart and the whole of the soul—with its intelligence, will and feeling—participate through devotion."

The Psalms are the songs of a worshipping community, not only of individuals, a community taken up into love and adoration of God, yet acknowledging all the unwelcome and unpalatable aspects of the world we live in—individual suffering and corporate disaster, betrayal, injustice and sin. They are cries of pain as well as of joy, of bewilderment as well as trust, laments for God's apparent absence as well as celebrations of his presence. They are a challenge to find words to praise God in all circumstances. Your letter, in opening up for us some of the riches of the devotion of the Qur'an helps us appreciate afresh the riches of the Psalms. Perhaps in future the statement in the Qur'an, *"to David We gave the Psalms"* (4:163), might encourage us to explore further together our traditions and practices of praise and how in our diverse ways we seek to bring to God the whole of our human imagination and sensitivity in a unified act of praise.

The Psalms teach us that the name of God, God's full, personal, mysterious and unsearchable reality, is to be continually celebrated and the life of faith is to be filled with praise of God.[19] We love God first not for what he has done for us but 'for his name's sake'—because of

[19] Psalm 145:1 quoted above and, e.g., Psalm 113:1-6:
[1]Praise the LORD! Praise, O servants of the LORD; praise the name of the LORD.
[2]Blessed be the name of the LORD from this time on and for evermore.
[3]From the rising of the sun to its setting the name of the LORD is to be praised.
[4]The LORD is high above all nations, and his glory above the heavens.
[5]Who is like the LORD our God, who is seated on high,
[6]who looks far down on the heavens and the earth?

who God *is*. Even in the midst of terrible suffering or doubt it is possible, with Job, to say: "**Blessed be the name of the Lord**" (Job 1:21). In the prayer which Jesus taught to his disciples the leading petition is: "**Hallowed be your name**" (Matthew 6:9). This means not only that honouring and blessing God is the first and most comprehensive activity of those who follow Jesus; it also encourages Christians to give thanks for all the ways in which God's name is proclaimed as holy and to be held in honour—by Christians, by people of other faiths and indeed by the whole order of creation which proclaims the glory of God.[20]

> [9] **Mountains and all hills, fruit trees and all cedars!**
>
> [10] **Wild animals and all cattle, creeping things and flying birds!**
>
> [11] **Kings of the earth and all peoples, princes and all rulers of the earth!**
>
> [12] **Young men and women alike, old and young together!**
>
> [13] **Let them praise the name of the LORD, for his name alone is exalted; his glory is above earth and heaven.** (Psalm 148)

So, with all creation, we join together in this chorus of universal praise – echoed so vividly in some of the phrases quoted in your letter.[21,22] Jesus said "**I came that they** [we] **may have life, and have it abundantly**." (John 10:10) and offering such praise and honour to God is in many ways the heart of the new life. The conviction that the love of God lives in us through his Holy Spirit, that to God we owe the very breath of life within us, is the motivation for our response to God's

[20] Amongst many examples see Psalm 148:9-13 quoted above and
[1]**The heavens are telling the glory of God; and the firmament proclaims his handiwork.**
[2]**Day to day pours forth speech, and night to night declares knowledge.** (Psalm 19.1-2)

[21] "The words: *His is the sovereignty and His is the praise and He hath power over all things,* when taken all together, remind Muslims that just as everything in creation glorifies God, everything that is in their souls must be devoted to God: *All that is in the heavens and all that is in the earth glorifieth God...* (al-Taghabun, 64:1)".

[22] "God says in one of the very first revelations in the Holy Qur'an: *So invoke the Name of thy Lord and devote thyself to Him with a complete devotion* (al-Muzzammil, 73:8)".

love—both in loving God and loving neighbour. We know from personal experience that true love can not be commanded or conditioned; it is freely given and received. Our love of God, as already indicated, is first and foremost a response of gratitude enabling us to grow in holiness—to become closer and closer in our actions and thoughts to the complete self-giving that always exists perfectly in God's life and is shown in the life and death of Jesus.

Towards this fullness we are all called to travel and grow and we shall want to learn from you more about the understandings of love of God in Islam as we continue this journey, exploring the implications of this love in our lives and our relationships with each other. Jesus, on the night before he died, said, **"I give you a new commandment, that you love one another. Just as I have loved you, you also should love one another."** (John 13:34). Responding to this new commandment to dwell in the love he bears us means allowing it to transform us and, so transformed, to love others—irrespective of their response.

Love of Our Neighbour

> [Jesus said:] **'You have heard that it was said, "You shall love your neighbour and hate your enemy." But I say to you, Love your enemies and pray for those who persecute you, so that you may be children of your Father in heaven; for he makes his sun rise on the evil and on the good, and sends rain on the righteous and on the unrighteous. For if you love those who love you, what reward do you have? Do not even the tax-collectors do the same? And if you greet only your brothers and sisters, what more are you doing than others? Do not even the Gentiles do the same? Be perfect, therefore, as your heavenly Father is perfect.'** (Matthew 5:43-48)

We support the clear affirmation in your letter, through texts from the Qur'an and the Bible, of the importance of love for the neighbour. Indeed, your letter can be considered an encouraging example of this love. We endorse the emphasis on generosity and self-sacrifice, and trust that these might be mutual marks of our continuing relationship with each other. The section in your letter on love for the neighbour is relatively brief, so we look forward to developing further the ways in which the theme is worked out within our traditions. We believe we have much to learn from each other in this matter, drawing on resources of wisdom, law, prophecy, poetry and narrative, both within and beyond our canonical scriptures[23] to help each other come to a richer vision of being loving neighbours today.

For Christians, our love for God is always a response to God's prior free love of humankind (and all creation). Enabled by this gift of love, our love becomes by grace something that mirrors the character of God's love and so can be offered to the stranger and the other. A full exploration of the significance of this will only be possible as we grow in our encounters together but, within the confines of this letter, we would want to draw attention to two aspects of the love of neighbour that are important for Christians.

The first is illustrated in St Luke's gospel when Jesus, having given the Dual Commandment of love as the response to the question "what must I do to inherit eternal life?" goes on to tell the parable of the Good Samaritan when asked to explain "who is my neighbour?"[24] Commentary on this parable frequently points to the way in which Jesus challenges the assumptions of the question; instead of defining a necessarily limited group of people who might fit the category of 'neighbours' to whom love should be shown, he speaks of the need to prove ourselves neighbours by compassion to whoever is before us in need or pain, whether or not they are akin to us, approved by

[23] The stories of saints and other exemplary people can often be of special value in conveying the quality of love.

[24] **Just then a lawyer stood up to test Jesus. 'Teacher,' he said, 'what must I do to inherit eternal life?'**
26He said to him, 'What is written in the law? What do you read there?'
27He answered, 'You shall love the Lord your God with all your heart, and with all your soul, and with all your strength, and with all your mind; and your neighbour as yourself.'
28And he said to him, 'You have given the right answer; do this, and you will live.'
29 But wanting to justify himself, he asked Jesus, 'And who is my neighbour?'
30Jesus replied, 'A man was going down from Jerusalem to Jericho, and fell into the hands of robbers, who stripped him, beat him, and went away, leaving him half dead.
31Now by chance a priest was going down that road; and when he saw him, he passed by on the other side.
32So likewise a Levite, when he came to the place and saw him, passed by on the other side.
33But a Samaritan while travelling came near him; and when he saw him, he was moved with pity.
34He went to him and bandaged his wounds, having poured oil and wine on them. Then he put him on his own animal, brought him to an inn, and took care of him.
35The next day he took out two denarii, gave them to the innkeeper, and said, "Take care of him; and when I come back, I will repay you whatever more you spend."
36Which of these three, do you think, was a neighbour to the man who fell into the hands of the robbers?'
37He said, 'The one who showed him mercy.' Jesus said to him, 'Go and do likewise.' (Luke 10:25-37)

us, safe for us to be with or whatever else. Such neighbourliness will mean crossing religious and ethnic divisions and transcending ancient enmities. So the 'neighbour' of the original Torah is defined by Jesus as whoever the 'other' is who specifically and concretely requires self-forgetful attention and care in any moment. Thus to be a neighbour is a challenge that continually comes at us in new ways. We cannot define its demands securely in advance; it demands that we be ready to go beyond the boundaries of our familiar structures of kinship and obligation, whether these are local, racial or religious. For that reason—developing a helpful symbolic reading of this parable—Christian thinkers have often said that Jesus himself is our first 'neighbour', the one who comes alongside every human being in need.[25] We look forward to the opportunity to explore with you how this teaching about being a neighbour relates to the Qur'anic imperative to care for neighbour and stranger (an imperative that seems to be derived here from the worship of God).[26]

The second aspect, already mentioned above, is Jesus' teaching about the love of those who do not necessarily love you. We have quoted above the version attributed to St Matthew, but the Gospel according to Luke contains a similar passage:

> **If anyone strikes you on the cheek, offer the other also; and from anyone who takes away your coat do not withhold even your shirt. Give to everyone who begs from you; and if anyone takes away your goods, do not ask for them again. Do to others as you would have them do to you... But love your enemies, do good, and lend, expecting nothing in return. Your reward will be great, and you will be children of the Most High; for he is kind to the ungrateful and the wicked. Be merciful, just as your Father is merciful.** (Luke 6:29-31,35-36)

This radical teaching, which Jesus presents precisely as a higher interpretation of what it means to love the neighbour, is grounded, as

[25] Cf. Karl Barth's similarly reversing reading of this parable: 'The primary and true form of the neighbour is that he faces us as the bearer and representative of the divine compassion,' *Church Dogmatics*, volume I/2, eds. G. W. Bromiley and T. F. Torrance (Edinburgh: T&T Clark, 1956) p. 416.

[26] "*Worship God; join nothing with Him. Be good to your parents, to relatives, to orphans, to the needy, to neighbours near and far, to travellers in need, and to your slaves.*" (4:36)

we have seen, in the way in which God loves. It teaches us to recognise as neighbour even those who set themselves against us. This is partly required by humility before the design of God in history and the limited nature of our perspective, for we do not know, as Christians have often said, who among those who confront us in hostility today will turn out to be our friends on the last day, when we stand before our Judge. It is partly, too, 'that we may be children of our Father in heaven',[27] learning to share the perspective of God, who reaches out and seeks to win all his creatures to his love, even those who turn away from it. This resonates with what is said in the Qur'an: "*God may still bring about affection between you and your present enemies—God is all powerful, God is most forgiving and merciful*" (Al-Mumtahana 60:7). Where love replaces enmity we can recognise the work and way of God.

Seeking the Common Good in the Way of God

"**Love works no ill to his neighbour.**" (Romans 13:10)

"**Let brotherly love continue. Be not forgetful to entertain strangers.**" (Hebrews 13:1-2)

There are many practical implications that flow from our understandings of love of God and love of neighbour, including those mentioned in your letter regarding peacemaking, religious freedom and the avoidance of violence.[28] In response we should like to offer a vision,

[27] Cf. Matthew 5:45.

[28] Among the many items for this agenda one respondent, Colin Chapman, suggests: **Our histories**: we need to recognise the legacy of 1400 years of sometimes difficult relationships between Christians and Muslims. Both faiths have at different times and in different places been associated with conquest and empire. And while there have been times of peaceful co-existence, conflicts between Muslims and Christians in the past (and present) have left their mark on the collective memory of both communities. **The wide variety of reasons for tensions in different situations today**: while there are some common factors in all situations where Muslims and Christians live side by side, in each situation there is also likely to be a unique set of factors—political, economic, cultural or social—which contribute to these tensions. **Christians and Muslims as minorities**: we recognise that 25% of Muslims worldwide are living in minority situations, and Christians also in many parts of the world find themselves as minorities. In contexts like these both Christians and Muslims face similar dilemmas and may have more in common with each other than with their secular neighbours. **The Israeli-Palestinian conflict** is at or near the top of the list of issues that concern both Christians and Muslims all over the world. This conflict is quite unique in the way that religion and politics are so thoroughly intertwined. Christian and Muslim

grounded in absolute faithfulness to our respective religious convictions, that we believe we can share in offering to our fellow believers and our neighbours (in the widest sense).

To believe in an absolute religious truth is to believe that the object of our belief is not vulnerable to the contingencies of human history: God's mind and character cannot be changed by what happens here in the world. Thus an apparent defeat in the world for our belief cannot be definitive; God does not fail just because we fail to persuade others or because our communities fail to win some kind of power. If we were to believe that our failure is a failure or defeat for God, then the temptation will be to seek for any means possible to avoid such an outcome. But that way lies terrorism and religious war and persecution. The idea that any action, however extreme or disruptive or even murderous, is justified if it averts failure or defeat for a particular belief or a particular religious group is not really consistent with the conviction that our failure does not mean God's failure. Indeed, it reveals a fundamental lack of conviction in the eternity and sufficiency of the object of faith.

Religious violence suggests an underlying religious insecurity. When different communities have the same sort of conviction of the absolute truth of their perspective, there is certainly an intellectual and spiritual challenge to be met; but the logic of this belief ought to make it plain that there can be no justification for the sort of violent contest in which any means, however inhuman, can be justified by appeal to the need to 'protect God's interests'. Even to express it in those terms is to show how absurd it is. The eternal God cannot need

leaders therefore have a special responsibility both to educate their own communities about 'the things that make for peace' and to appeal to their political leaders to work for a just resolution of the conflict.Love of the neighbour, as *A Common Word* suggests, provides a firm basis on which to address many of these immediate issues that affect Christian-Muslim relations all over the world. When Muslims point to the saying of Muhammad "None of you has faith until you love for your brother (or neighbour) what you love for yourself", Christians point to the Golden Rule as taught by Jesus: "**In everything do to others as you would have them do to you; for this is the law and the prophets**" (Matthew 7:12). This must mean in practice, for example, that when western Christians try to put themselves in the shoes of the Christians in Egypt and reflect on how they would like to be treated in that minority situation, this should affect the way that they think about Muslim minorities in the West. The principle of reciprocity seems to many to be a natural expression of love of the neighbour, since it means wanting for our neighbours what we want for ourselves. Its acceptance by both Christians and Muslims would help to resolve many of the tensions experienced by both Christian and Muslim minorities.

'protection' by the tactics of human violence. This point is captured in the words of Jesus before the Roman governor: "**My kingdom is not of this world. If it were, my servants would fight**" (John 19.36).

So we can conclude that the more we as people of genuine faith are serious about the truth of our convictions, the more likely we will be to turn away from violence in the name of faith; to trust that God, the truly real, will remain true, divine and unchanging, whatever the failures and successes of human society and history. And we will be aware that to try and compel religious allegiance through violence is really a way of seeking to replace divine power with human; hence the Qur'anic insistence that there can be no compulsion in matters of religious faith (al-Baqarah, 2:256[29]) and the endorsement in your letter of "freedom of religion". It is crucial to faith in a really existing and absolute transcendent agency that we should understand it as being what it is quite independently of any lesser power: the most disturbing form of secularisation is when this is forgotten or misunderstood.

This has, indeed, been forgotten or misunderstood in so many contexts over the millennia. Religious identity has often been confused with cultural or national integrity, with structures of social control, with class and regional identities, with empire; and it has been imposed in the interest of all these and other forms of power. Despite Jesus' words in John's gospel, Christianity has been promoted at the point of the sword and legally supported by extreme sanctions[30]; despite the Qur'anic axiom, Islam has been supported in the same way, with extreme penalties for abandoning it, and civil disabilities for those outside the faith. There is no religious tradition whose history is exempt from such temptation and such failure.

What we need as a vision for our dialogue is to break the current cycles of violence, to show the world that faith and faith alone can truly ground a commitment to peace which definitively abandons the tempting but lethal cycle of retaliation in which we simply imitate each other's violence.[31] Building on our understanding of God's love

[29] *There is no compulsion in religion.*

[30] There has been, and continues to be, a tradition within Christianity that has argued the moral rightness of using force in certain carefully defined circumstances, most notably through the application of the "just war" criteria formulated by St Augustine of Hippo and developed by St Thomas Aquinas.

[31] And here we must recognise, in the words of the initial reflections on *A Common Word* offered by Daniel Madigan SJ "... an honest examination of conscience will not permit us to forget that our future is not threatened only by conflict

for us and, in response, our love for God and neighbour we can speak of a particular quality to the Christian approach to peace and peacemaking: the moment of *unconditioned* positive response, the risk of offering something to one whom you have no absolutely secure reason to trust.

Many Christians have said that your letter represents such an offering—a gift with no certainty of what might be the response. We want to acknowledge the courage of such a move, and respond in kind. Let us explore together how this dimension of Christian language, born of the unconditional and self-sacrificial love of neighbour, can be correlated with the language of the Qur'an.

Such an approach can take us beyond a bland affirmation that we are at peace with those who are at peace with us to a place where our religious convictions can be a vehicle for creating peace where it is absent.

Such a commitment to seek together the common good can, we are convinced, sit alongside a fundamental recognition that, even with our commitments to love God and neighbour, we cannot expect to find some 'neutral' positions beyond the traditions of our faith that would allow us to broker some sort of union between our diverse convictions. Far from being a cause for concern, holding fast to our truth claims whilst rejecting violence does two very positive things at once. First it affirms the transcendent source of faith: it says that our views are not just human constructions which we can abandon when they are inconvenient. Second, by insisting that no other values, no secular values, are absolute, it denies to all other systems of values any justification for uncontrolled violence. Transcendent values can be defended through violence only by those who do not fully under-

between us. Over the centuries of undeniable conflict and contestation between members of our two traditions, each group has had its own internal conflicts that have claimed and continue to claim many more lives than interconfessional strife. More Muslims are killed daily by other Muslims than by Christians or anyone else. The huge numbers who went to their deaths in the Iran-Iraq war of the 1980's were virtually all Muslims. Scarcely any of the tens of millions of Christians who have died in European wars over the centuries were killed by Muslims. The greatest shame of the last century was the killing of millions of Jews by Christians conditioned by their own long tradition of anti-Semitism and seduced by a virulently nationalist and racist new ideology. The last 15 years in Africa have seen millions of Christians slaughtered in horrendous civil wars by their fellow believers... So let us not be misled into thinking either that Muslim-Christian conflict is the world's greatest conflict, or even that war is the most serious threat to the human future."

stand their transcendent character; and if no other value is absolute, no other value can claim the right to unconditional defence by any means and at all costs.

So, even if we accept that our systems of religious belief cannot be reconciled by 'rational' argument because they depend on the gift of revelation, we rule out, by that very notion, any assumption that coercive human power is the ultimate authority and arbiter in our world. Given, as we have acknowledged, that Christian history contains too many examples of Christians betraying that initial turning away from the cycle of retaliation, we can only put forward such a vision in the form of a challenge to Christians as much as Muslims: how did we ever come to think that the truly transcendent can ever be imagined or proclaimed in a pattern of endless and sterile repetition of force?

And here we can together suggest a way in which religious plurality can be seen as serving the cause of social unity and acting as a force for the common good. As people of faith, we can never claim that social harmony can be established by uncontrolled coercive power. This means that we are not obliged to defend and argue for the legitimacy and righteousness of any social order. As the world now is, diverse religious traditions very frequently inhabit one territory, one nation, one social unit (and that may be a relatively small unit like a school, or a housing co-operative or even a business). In such a setting, we cannot avoid the pragmatic and secular question of 'common security': what is needed for our convictions to flourish is bound up with what is needed for the convictions of other groups to flourish. We learn that we can best defend ourselves by defending others. In a plural society, Christians secure their religious liberty by advocacy for the liberty of people of other faiths to have the same right to be heard in the continuing conversation about the direction and ethos of society.

And we can extend this still further. If we are in the habit of defending each other, we ought to be able to learn to defend other groups and communities as well. We can together speak for those who have no voice or leverage in society—for the poorest, the most despised, the least powerful, for women and children, for migrants and minorities; and even to speak together for that great encompassing reality which has no 'voice' or power of its own—our injured and abused material environment, which both our traditions of faith tell us we should honour and care for.

Our voice in the conversation of society will be the stronger for being a joint one. If we are to be true to the dual commandment of love, we need to find ways of being far more effective in influencing our societies to follow the way of God in promoting that which leads to human flourishing—honesty and faithfulness in public and private relationships, in business as in marriage and family life; the recognition that a person's value is not an economic matter; the clear recognition that neither material wealth nor entertainment can secure a true and deep-rooted human fulfilment.

Seeking Together in the Way of God

A Common Word Between Us and You issues a powerful call to dialogue and collaboration between Christians and Muslims. A great deal is already happening in this sphere on many levels, but the very wide geographical (43 countries) and theological diversity represented among the signatories of your letter provides a unique impetus to deepen and extend the encounters. As part of the common shape and structure of our language about God we can acknowledge a shared commitment to truth and a desire to discern how our lives may come to be lived in accordance with eternal truth. As we have noted above, the Christian understanding of love, coupled with our common acknowledgement of the absolute transcendence of the divine, encourages us towards a vision of radical and transformative non-violence. We are committed to reflecting and working together, with you and all our human neighbours, with a view both to practical action and service and to a long term dedication to all that will lead to a true common good for human beings before God.

This is a good moment to attempt to coordinate a way forward for our dialogue. We suggest an approach drawing on *Dialogue and Proclamation*, a 1991 Vatican document whose four categories of inter-religious dialogue have been found widely helpful. They are:

the dialogue of life, "where people strive to live in an open and neighbourly spirit";

the dialogue of action, "in which Christians and others collaborate for the integral development and liberation of people";

the dialogue of theological exchange, "where specialists seek to deepen their understanding of their respective religious heritages"; and

the dialogue of religious experience, "where persons rooted in their own religious traditions share their spiritual riches".

This typology can be applied more generally to the whole pattern of encounter between Christians and Muslims, even where this is not directly described as 'dialogue'.

Three imperatives are suggested by this:

to strengthen grass-roots partnerships and programmes between our communities that will work for justice, peace and the common good of human society the world over;

to intensify the shared theological discussions and researches of religious leaders and scholars who are seeking clearer insight into divine truth, and to realise this through building and sustaining of groups marked by a sense of collegiality, mutual esteem, and trust;[32]

to deepen the appreciation of Christian and Muslim believers for each other's religious practice and experience, as they come to recognise one another as people whose lives are oriented towards God in love.[33]

These different kinds of encounter need to be held together to ensure a balanced and effective pattern of encounter. The approach of your letter shows the importance of shared and attentive study of Biblical and Qur'anic texts as a way of ensuring both that all dimensions of encounter are present and also that Christians and Muslims are held accountable to, and draw on the riches of, their respective traditions of faith whilst recognising the limitations—at least initially—in our ability to comment authoritatively on the others' scriptures.[34]

[32] While such colloquia should be characterised by a high degree of academic rigour, they should also draw on and express the personal commitment of religious leaders and scholars to their respective faiths.

[33] This will require spending time in each other's presence, exploring the depth of each other's spirituality, and acknowledging both the variety and the depth of prayer, remembrance and celebration in both faiths.

[34] The Christian Bible, Old and New Testaments together, forms a large narrative (with, admittedly, many subordinate parts some of which do not well fit the 'narrative' model) from creation to new creation, from the Garden of Eden to the New Jerusalem which comes down from heaven to earth. Within this narrative, Jesus Christ is presented as the climax of the story of the world's creation on the one

As we noted earlier, the role of the Qu'ran in Islam is not really parallel to the role of the Bible in Christianity. For Christians, God's Word was made flesh in Jesus Christ. Our understanding of the Scriptures is that they witness to and draw their authority from Christ, describing the witness of prophets and apostles to his saving work. They are the voice of his living Spirit who, Christians believe, dwells among us and within us. Nevertheless, for us as for you, reading the Scriptures is a constant source of inspiration, nurture and correction, and this makes it very appropriate for Christians and Muslims to listen to one another, and question one another, in the course of reading and interpreting the texts from which we have learned of God's will and purposes. And for Christians and Muslims together addressing our scriptures in this way, it is essential also to take account of the place of the Jewish people and of the Hebrew scriptures in our encounter, since we both look to our origins in that history of divine revelation and action.

The use of scriptures in inter-religious dialogue has considerable potential, but there are also risks in this approach when we think we know or understand another's sacred texts but in fact are reading them exclusively through our own spectacles. We hope that one early outcome of studying and discussing together will be to work out wise guidelines, practices and educational resources for this element of our engagement.

Given the variety of forms of encounter which are to be held together as we deepen our engagement with each other, we can identify three main outcomes which we might seek together. They will depend on the establishment and maintenance of credible and durable structures of collegiality, trust and respect between key individuals and communities in our two faiths. The three outcomes are:

> Maintaining and strengthening the momentum of what is already happening in Christian-Muslim encounter. An important stream flowing into this will be the continuing conversations around your letter and the Christian responses to it. Reach-

hand and of the call of Abraham on the other: the stories of Jesus are not *just* 'stories of Jesus' but 'stories of Jesus seen as the fulfilment of covenant and creation'. The multiple teachings which are found variously throughout the Bible—doctrine about God, rules for behaviour, religious practices etc.—are set, and best understood, within that overall story. It would be worth exploring in some detail how Muslims see these aspects of Christian scripture and whether there are ways in which such a perception would create new kinds of possibilities for dialogue.

ing back before that also, there has been a growing corpus of action and reflection in this area at least from *Nostra Aetate* (1965) onwards. The recent gathering of Muslim religious leaders and scholars in Mecca and the subsequent convening of a conference in Madrid, for example, is another promising development. It is important that any new initiatives acknowledge this wider picture of Christian-Muslim encounter, and position themselves in relation to it, learning from both its achievements and set-backs.

Finding safe spaces within which the differences – as well as the convergences - between Christians and Muslims can be honestly and creatively articulated and explored. Our two faiths have differed deeply on points of central importance to both of us, points of belief as well as points of practice. It is essential for the health of our encounter that we should find ways of talking freely yet courteously about those differences; indeed, honesty of this kind has been described as the most certain sign of maturity in dialogue.

Ensuring that our encounters are not for the sake of participants alone, but are capable of having an influence which affects people more widely—Christians and Muslims at the level of all our local communities, and also those engaged in the wider realities of our societies and our world. Seeking the common good is a purpose around which Christians and Muslims can unite, and in leads us into all kinds of complex territory as we seek to find ways of acting effectively in the world of modern global and democratic politics.

Within the wide diversity of patterns of encounter and participation, it will be desirable to establish some broad priorities in order to keep Christian-Muslim relations focused and effective around a number of core themes. Again, three steps seem worth establishing here:

First, there is an urgent need in both our traditions for education about one another. We are all influenced by prejudices and misunderstandings inherited from the past—and often renewed in the present through the power of media stereotyping. Teaching and learning about the reality and diversity of Islam as Muslims practise their faith should be a priority as important to Christians as understanding of actual Christianity should be to Muslims. In concrete terms, such educational programmes might be initially be focused on those preparing clergy and imams respectively for public inter-faith roles and on those providing religious education to young people.

Second, opportunities for lived encounter with people of different faiths, both within and across national boundaries, need to be multiplied and developed in an atmosphere of trust and respect. These should take place on many different levels and in many different settings. Such opportunities might usefully be focused on educational projects, efforts towards the attainment of the Millennium Development Goals and shared work for reconciliation in situations of conflict and historic enmities.

Finally, for encounters to be sustainable over a long period of time, there needs to be commitment to the process and to one another on the part of all participants. Such a commitment, growing into affection, respect, collegiality and friendship, will be an expression of love of neighbour; it will also be done in love for God and in response to God's will.

We believe that *A Common Word Between Us and You* opens the way for these steps to be approached in a new spirit. The limitations of making further statements or sending further letters in advance of meeting together are obvious, however good and friendly the intentions. We greatly look forward therefore to discussing face to face some of the questions arising from these exchanges of letters, exploring—as was said earlier—both the concepts that have been sketched and the new possibilities for creative work together for the good of our world.

So to your invitation to enter more deeply into dialogue and collaboration as a part of our faithful response to the revelation of God's purpose for humankind, we say: Yes! Amen.

The Word of God
The Bridge between Him, You and Us

by Seyyed Hossein Nasr

> *Say, O People of the Book! Come to a word common between us and you, that we shall worship none but God, and shall not associate aught with Him, and shall not take one another as lords apart from God.* (Quran, 3:65)

The common word to which the chapter of the Quran "The House of 'Imrān" refers and from which the title of the document "A Common Word between Us and You" has been taken has been interpreted by such major traditional commentators as Zamakhshahrī, Fakhr al-Dīn al-Rāzī and Ibn 'Arabī as referring to Divine Unity or *al-Tawḥīd*. Surely this is its basic meaning as the Unity of the Divine Principle is what is common between all the Us's and all the You's who follow the sacred teachings at the heart of all authentic religions. The common word means not only the acceptance of Divine Unity but also attachment to the One with our whole being and therefore including love of the One and moreover the love of His creation or the neighbor, for the neighbor comes from the One and returns to It. The common word stated in the Quran contains, therefore, within itself implicitly the two commandments of Christ announced in chapter 12 of the Gospel of Mark in the New Testament. The consequence of our realization of our ontological dependence upon the One as absolute regarding Him and also regarding what issues from Him in light of the ontological dependence of all of creation upon Him cannot but include His two commandments.

This paper was presented at the Yale University conference, "Loving God and Neighbor in Word and Deed," July 2008.

There is furthermore a second possible interpretation of "the common word" which can bring you and us, or more particularly Christians and Muslims, even closer together by embracing the instrument or the means by which the One has revealed Himself to all of us, Christian and Muslim alike. The second interpretation has to do with the meaning of the term "word" itself. In the original Arabic of the verse from "The House of 'Imrān" the term that is used is *kalimah*. Now the Noble Quran is known among Muslims as *kalām Allāh* or *kalimat Allāh* meaning literally Word of God, while the term is also used in connection with Moses and Jesus. It is precisely this term that corresponds to the word *logos* in Christian Greek sources. Contrary to what some have claimed the doctrine of the logos exists as much in Islam as it does in Christianity albeit with different interpretations resulting from the different receptacles for which a religion is meant and also the diversity of Divine manifestations. As Islamic sources assert, *kullu yawmin Huwa fi 'l-sha'n*, that is, "every day He manifests Himself in a different state." Furthermore, while the Gospel of John asserts that it was by the Word that all things were made, the chapter *Yā Sīn* in the Quran exclaims that God said "be!" (*kun)* and there was. There is therefore again a similarity of cosmogonic function in the two religions as far as the Word is concerned.

Consequently, one can say that not only Divine Unity is a common word between us and you but that there is also a single *kalimah* or Logos in its principial reality in which we believe jointly, except that for you the Word is identified with Christ and for us with the Quran. It would bring us closer to each other if we realized that we are bound together not only by the doctrine of the One but also by the "doctrine of the Word" and if we fixed our gaze upon the metahistorical and principial Word/Logos and not upon one of its particular historical manifestations. There *were*, however, particular manifestations of this reality and hence the creation of Christianity and Islam, as well as other religions, especially Judaism if we confine ourselves within the Abrahamic family of religions, religions in which there are universal elements that unify and bind as well as formal aspects and particularities that separate. Needless to say different understandings of *kalimah* or *logos* have existed also within each tradition as we see in the formulation of different types of Christology and also different understandings of the meaning of the Quran as Word of God.

Obviously the common word as related to Divine Unity followed by the Word as *kalimah* or *Logos* in its metaphysical sense and the resulting love of God and neighbor are the most important elements that unify and bind us together. The traditional Catholic credo begins with *credo in unum Deum* which conveys the same meaning as *lā ilāha illa'Llāh*. Furthermore, we both accept the revelatory agency of the Word, however different might be our understanding of the form that the Word taken in this world and our interpretation of the process of revelation itself. From this similarity of doctrine issues the role played by Christ in Christianity as the perfect model to emulate, hence *imitatio Christi*, and the similar role played by the Prophet, the recipient of the Divine Word in Islam and the most perfect of men for Muslims although not considered as divine.

The list of similarities that bind us on the basis of these basic doctrines and that bring Christians and Muslims close together are too many to enumerate here. But let us mention just a few: acceptance of sacred scripture, belief in the reality and pre-eminence of the Spirit within and in the spiritual world beyond our subjectivism, the immortality of the soul, the efficacy of prayer and other religious rites, the necessity of the ethical character of human life here on earth and its consequences for life after death, ultimate judgment by God and eschatological realities, the reality of good and evil, interplay of the Mercy and Justice of God, the reflection of the Wisdom of God in His creation, and the existence of a path in this life on which to journey towards God as seen in the mysticism of the two religions. Even in matters of the relation of faith to reason, Christianity and Islam have developed many parallel doctrines. In fact in contrast to what some Christian sources have asserted, there is a Muslim parallel practically for *every* Christian position on the issue from Tertullian, St. Augustine, Anselm, and St. Thomas to Calvin and Luther and more recently Barth and Tillich, and vice versa. When on ponders even this incomplete list of shared elements, one becomes aware of how many basic doctrines and practices do indeed unite us, especially if our religions were to be compared to what is held to be central in secular society. Nor can one side accuse the other of being opposed to the use of reason in matters of religion or of lacking love.

Of course there are also walls that separate us. Otherwise Islam and Christianity would not have survived as separate religions as they have done providentially but the two seas would have commingled into a single ocean. God's Will seems to have commanded otherwise. In the *Mathnawī* of Jalāl al-Dīn Rūmī God addresses Moses and says, "Thou hast come to unify and not to separate." Surely, our task today and tomorrow is to follow this command but we cannot simply neglect the differences by pretending they do not exist. We hope that the common word between us and you will bring us closer together not because differences do not exist but will do so despite of their existence. As Frithjof Schuon once said, "Accord between religions is not possible in the human atmosphere but only in the Divine stratosphere." Our hope is that while being aware of the human atmosphere where different religious ideas and forms do exist as willed by God, we can ascend through the love and knowledge of God and also sapience to the stratosphere where we can reach accord.

Meanwhile in this human atmosphere where we reside we see such apparently insurmountable differences as the emphasis of Islam on Divine Unity and negation of Trinity (at least as understood in the Quran) and the Christian emphasis on the Trinity which is even transposed into the domain of Unity itself. We disagree on the episodes at the end of the life of Christ and of course his divinity in contrast to his being a major prophet of God. We do not see eye to eye about the relation between canonical law and secular law on the one hand and *al-Sharī'ah* and *al-qānūn* on the other. While much of our ethics is similar we do have different views concerning sexuality and its relation to original sin that is central to much of Christian thought but rejected by Islam.

In this context of similarities and contrasts we each follow the teachings of a religion that claims to have a universal message for the whole of humanity and this claim has played no small role in the long history of animosity between the two religions. It has led to religious wars, crusades, coercive missionary activity and much else that has colored and still colors the relation between the two religions. Christians accuse Muslims of violence without paying attention to their own history and to what the Native Americans of New England would have said about the relation of Christianity to violence had they survived to attend this conference. Muslims accuse Christians of not paying enough attention to the social teachings of religion based on justice while not pointing out sufficiently the unjust practices that go on in parts of the Islamic world. A number of people on both sides also tend to paint the other with the color of an extremist fringe, Christians using terrorism and Muslims the blasphemy against Islam, the Quran and the Prophet and what has come to be known more generally as Islamophobia. Needless to say both terrorism in the Islamic world and Islamophobia do remain real but they do not determine the whole reality of Islamic-Christian understanding. Meanwhile, both sides accuse the other of not practicing what they preach.

Yes, these and many other impediments have to be confronted head on and not simply ignored. On the social and political levels the two religions have to be also self-critical of their own societies and not simply surrender to the political forces of the two worlds in which they form a majority. On the theological level there must be in-depth dialogue if more external issues are to be solved. Without truth religious dialogue becomes simply political expediency and it is then better to leave it in the hands of diplomats rather than committed scholars of religion and theologians. Deep theological dialogue does not necessarily mean the surrender of one side to the other; it does, however, mean better understanding of the other and greater mutual respect. At least one can agree to disagree rather than casting anathema upon the other side. Of course the ideal would be to transcend the formal order altogether to reach the transcendent truth of which theological doctrines are so many crystallizations. That truth resides in the world of meaning beyond forms, in what Rūmī calls the "spiritual retreat of God." But until we get there we must be able to come together, to know each other, to love one another, and to face together the many challenges posed by a world based on the forgetfulness of God. And it is precisely in this situation that a common word between us and you can play such a crucial role if there is sincerity and correct intention on both sides.

In light of a long history of contentions and confrontations, of theological differences irreducible on the theological level and the need to realize this fact, and of the unprecedented global crisis in which accord or discord between religions has become crucial, it becomes clear why the common word between us and you is of such significance. Surely "the common word" is a most efficacious way to bring about amity between Christianity and Islam without either side sacrificing the truth upon which it stands. And what can be more important to a religion than truth without which religion divorces itself from its very source. Did not Christ call himself the Truth and is reference not made to God in the Quran as *al-Ḥaqq*, the Truth?

It is of the utmost importance for us assembled here to realize that "the common word" that we are asked to accept and share does not at the same time demand of us to forgo the truth or to relativize it in the name of religious accord as happens in so much of the shallow ecumenism prevalent today that is willing to sacrifice truth for the sake of expediency.

The necessity of acceptance of the two commandments of the love of God and of the neighbor on the basis of the saying of Christ and hence Christian truth is evident to Christians. As for Muslims, the two principles are mentioned in the Quran and *Ḥadīth* and their acceptance is therefore necessary and is moreover seen by Muslims to be based solidly on Islamic teachings. Furthermore, it must be remembered that according to Islamic beliefs what has been brought by an earlier prophet and not explicitly abrogated by a later revelation still stands as an expression of truth and God's commandment to and will for Muslims. In light of this belief, the two commandments of Christ are also commandments for Muslims even if they had been neither confirmed nor abrogated in the Quran and *Ḥadīth*. Christ is after all not only the founder of Christianity, but also a major Islamic prophet.

Coming now to the meaning of the two commandments, three related issues come to mind and need to be explained: the meaning of God, the meaning of love and the meaning of the love of God and neighbor. Without some accord on these issues, we would be attacked by those who stand against mutual harmony and comprehension on the subject of the very terms we are using in "the common word." There are already those on the Christian side who assert that the Christian God is not the same as Allah, who is an Arabic lunar deity or something like that. Such people who usually combine sheer ignorance with bigotry should attend a Sunday mass in Arabic in Bethlehem, Beirut, Amman or Cairo and see what Arabic term the Christians of these cities use for the Christian God. Nor is God simply to be identified with a member of the Christian Trinity as part of three divinities that some Muslims believe wrongly that Christians worship. Allah or God is none other than the One God of Abraham, Isaac, Ishmael, Moses, Jesus and Muhammad. In speaking of the love of God, let us not accuse each other of referring to different gods. How can one study the Bible, including both the Old and the New Testament, and the Quran, without accepting that we are all breathing throughout all the worlds created by these sacred scriptures within the same universe of Abrahamic monotheism? What could be more insidious or even demonic than trying to undercut the binding effect of Christ's two commandments by claiming that Christians and Muslims are referring to two different gods and not the single God "whose mercy embraces all," as the Quran asserts?

As for love, it is a reality that transcends whatever one writes about it. As Rūmī said, when it came to love the pen broke and the ink dried. And yet so much has been written about the subject. One can either write nothing or fill libraries about love but finally one must experience love to know what it is. Love attaches the lover to the beloved, carries the lover through dales and valleys of joy and sorrow and finally leads to a union that is also a kind of death for *amor est mors*. The love of God is not only the highest form of love but in reality the only love of which all other loves are but shadows. To love God fully is to give ourselves wholly to Him, body, soul and mind not to speak of will and intelligence. We must give up our limited ego as that which defines us. The end of such love is what the Christian mystics call mystical union and to which Sufis refer in a somewhat different language but which concerns the same reality as being consumed by the fire of love as a moth is immolated by the divine flame of the divine candle.

For the purpose of our present discourse in the same way that it is not necessary to enter into contentious theological discussions about the nature of God, there is no need to enter into an analysis of the modes, stages and states of love. Let us love God and leave the mystery of this attachment of each soul to its Creator to the Creator Himself. At all costs we should avoid considering our love of God to be superior to the love of the other for God. Such an illusory contention arises from our mistaking our own understanding of the love for God for that love itself and absolutizing that understanding and of thereby inflating our egos in the guise of religious devotion and righteousness. Let us love God and leave Him to decide on the intensity and sincerity of our loves as well as of our differing views of Him. The Quran invites Muslims explicitly to live at peace with followers of other religions and let God decide on the Day of Judgment concerning the truth or falsehood of wherein they differed.

As for the love of the neighbor, this command has been understood in a different manner over the ages. Today, it cannot include only our

Muslim neighbors for Muslims, Christian neighbors for Christians or Jewish neighbors for Jews. It must also include followers of other religious communities, even non-religious communities and especially the non-human world. In fact if Muslims and Christians, not to speak of other groups, do not extend their love of the neighbor to the natural world, the consequences of the environmental crisis, caused ultimately by the lack of love of the neighbor in its larger reality, will make other efforts more or less irrelevant.

The Quran asserts that God created all of humanity from a single soul (*nafs wāḥidah*). Nevertheless, strife even within a single family not to speak of between religions and nations continues to manifest itself. One might say that as a result of what Muslims call the fall (*hubūṭ*) and Christians original sin the state of confrontation and strife is endemic to the human condition. But God has also given us the means of transcending the abode of strife for one of peace, of overcoming that religious and ideological exclusivism which now endangers human existence in favor of that inclusivism of which we gathered here are partisans.

It is not, however, enough to speak of a common word between us and you or even to accept its tenets with our tongue. We must also have the correct intention and live these commandments within ourselves while setting examples for others. Let us love God with all our being which means also to accept His Unity and the unity of His Word that unite us. And let us love the neighbor, and more specifically our Muslim and Christian neighbors, not on the basis of mere sentimentality that can weaken or strengthen in time, but on the never changing foundation of the Truth.

To live fully as a Muslim or Christian does not require anything less of us than loving the neighbor, whether he or she be Muslim or Christian, and to ask not "is he or she one of us," but "is he or she one of His."

God as 'The Loving' in Islam[1]

by Reza Shah-Kazemi

This article addresses the question: to what extent can God be described as 'The Loving' in the Islamic tradition? Quite apart from its intrinsic importance in terms of the Islamic conception of God, it is a question that has acquired extrinsic, quasi-political dimensions in the light of the recent discussions surrounding the historic 'A Common Word' initiative launched in Amman in 2007.[2] In essence, this was a call from Muslim scholars to the heads of all the major Christian denominations, inviting them to engage in dialogue, on the basis of what is 'common' to both traditions, and which might be said to constitute the heart of religion as such: love of God and love of the neighbour. Without pretending to reduce the diversity of religious traditions to this simple formula, the letter invited Christian leaders to engage in amicable dialogue on all relevant issues, including irreducible theological differences, but to do so within a framework defined by the principle of love, at once divine and human. This principle of love was deemed to constitute the indisputable common ground of Islam, Christianity and, indeed, all revealed religions. However, among the Christian voices critical of this initiative, one encountered the following objection: the Muslims do not place love at the centre of their faith as we Christians do; they do not see God primarily as love, as we do; the God in whom Muslims believe is a God of anger not love. According to this caricature, all too prevalent in the West, the very notion of a loving God in Islam is a contradiction in terms: *Allāh* is conceived by Muslims as utterly remote and aloof from his creation, so it is argued, his inaccessibility being the very ransom of his absoluteness. Therefore Allāh is but a transcendent Lawgiver, at best, an arbitrary dictator at worst. This caricature is then contrasted with the God in whom Christians believe, a God whose love is so

1 This is an expanded version of a paper presented at the conference 'Loving God and Neighbor in Word and Deed', Yale University, July 25, 2008.

2 See www.acommonword.com for the document itself, and the responses thereto by a large number of Christian scholars, leaders, churches and organisations.

clearly enunciated in the famous words of St John's Gospel: 'For God so loved the world, that He gave His only-begotten Son, that whosoever believeth in him should not perish, but have everlasting life.' (John, 3:16) Whereas God's love is seen as absolute and unconditional in Christianity, it is seen by Muslims—if it is deemed to be seen by them at all—as strictly conditional: Allāh only loves those who submit to him.

In addressing the theme of God as 'The Loving' in Islam, then, this critique will also be addressed, albeit indirectly. The first part of the paper will look at the question of divine love from the point of view of theology and on the basis of a *prima facie* reading of the Qur'ān. The second moves from theology to spirituality, addressing the theme of divine love through the discourse of Sufism. In the third section the mystical speculations of the Sufis are seen to be grounded in a spiritual assimilation of the message of the Qur'ān and of the Prophet; here the all-encompassing nature of loving compassion, or compassionate love, *raḥma*, will be shown to be at the very heart of the Islamic conception of the divine nature. Finally, in the fourth section, the ultimate mystical implications of divine love are presented with reference to the principle of *walāya* or sanctity.

1. The Theological 'Problem' of Love

God is described in the Qur'ān as 'the Loving', *al-Wadūd*, and as He is qualified by the quality of love (*ḥubb*), in the Qur'ān. First, as regards the attribute *al-Wadūd*, we have the following two verses:

'And He is the Forgiving, the Loving' (85:14).

'Ask forgiveness of your Lord, then turn to Him repentant.
Truly my Lord is Merciful, Loving' (11:90).

It is important to note that in both places, the quality of divine love is linked with that of mercy and forgiveness. As will be seen in the following parts of this paper, this interpenetration of love and mercy is of utmost significance in the Islamic conception of God's love for His creation.

Although the name 'The Lover', *al-Muḥibb*, is not normally given as one of the ninety-nine names of God, the Qur'ān refers to God as 'loving' (*yuḥibbu*) in many places and in several respects. Thus, Fakhr al-Dīn al-Rāzi, one of the most important of the classical commentators, states in his comment on *al-Wadūd* in 85:14, that the meaning of this name is *al-Muḥibb*, and adds that this is the view of the majority of the commentators.[3] He adds that ascribing this quality of love (*ḥubb*) to God as al-Wadūd is based on intellectual evidence: God loves that which is good; and good is that which is required essentially (*muqtaḍā bi'l-dhāt*); evil, on the other hand, is but accidentally required. Every good thing is thus beloved by God on account of its essentiality. He also states that al-Wadūd can be understood in the passive sense, as the verbal noun *fa'ūl* can be understood in the sense of a *maf'ūl* (passive) form; he gives as examples the word *rakūb*, meaning mount, (that which is mounted), from the root *rakiba*, to ride; and *ḥalūb*, a cow (that which is milked), from the root *ḥalaba*, to milk. The meaning of *al-Wadūd* can thus also be 'The Beloved': God is beloved by His righteous slaves, according to al-Rāzī, 'who love Him on account of what they know of His perfections, those pertaining to His Essence, His Qualities, and His Acts.'

Al-Ṭabarī, in his seminal commentary, likewise refers to the principle of *maḥabba*, love, joining it with that of *maghfira* (forgiveness), as an explanation of the meaning of God as *al-Wadūd*. He also refers to an interpretation according to which the two names in 85:15, *al-Ghafūr, al-Wadūd*, together mean: *al-Ḥabīb*, the Beloved.[4]

In respect of God's love as *ḥubb*, we find that God is described as loving (*yuḥibbu*) eight types of people: the virtuous (*al-muḥsinīn*) (2:195 et passim); those who are repentant (*al-tawwābīn*) (2:222); those who purify themselves (*al-mutaṭahhirīn*) (2:222); the pious (*al-muttaqīn*) (3:76 et passim); those who have patience (*al-ṣābirīn*) (3:146); those who trust in Him (*al-mutawakkilīn*) (3:159); the just (*al-muqsiṭīn*) (5:42 et passim); those who fight for His sake (*yuqātilūna fī sabīlihi*) (6:14).[5] By contrast He is described in many verses as 'not loving' the disbelievers, the rebellious, the vicious, the proud, and so on.

This initial view of God as 'the Loving' reveals but a superficial apprehension of divine love, for the love in question appears not very different from human love: God, just like us, loves those who are good and does not love those who are bad. He promises to love those who

[3] Fakhr al-Dīn al-Rāzī, *al-Tafsīr al-kabīr* (Beirut: Dār Iḥyā᾽ al-Turāth al-ʿArabī, 2001), vol. 11, p.114.

[4] *Jāmi' al-bayān* (Beirut: Dār Iḥyā᾽ al-Turāth al-ʿArabī, 2001), vol. 30, p.169.

[5] A verse much commented upon by the Sufis refers to God bringing forth 'a people whom He loves and who love Him' (5:54).

follow the Prophet: 'Say [O Prophet]: If you love God, follow me. God will love you' (3:31).

It is on such a casual perusal of the Qur'ānic view of divine love that the outside observer might infer that for Muslims, God's love is conditional, it is contingent upon particular human acts and qualities, rather than being an essential aspect of God, manifested in a manner at once universal and unconditional. God's love appears to be given as a reward for the righteous and denied as a punishment to the sinners. While this cannot be disputed on its own level, it certainly does not exhaust the nature of the Islamic conception of divine love. The surface or immediate meaning of the verses cited pertains, in like fashion, to the surface or immediate manifestations of divine love within the created order. What remains to be discovered, beneath the surface of these verses, which yield only an initial starting point for exploration, is what the true nature of divine love is, and how this is related, not just to specific manifestations of God's love, but rather, to the very substance of manifestation itself—the whole of the created realm.

If the classical commentaries are consulted on these verses, the picture of divine love that emerges is not, however, substantially altered, for the commentators as a rule focus on the moral imperatives which flow from these verses, and stress the need for each individual to shed all blameworthy qualities and adopt the praiseworthy ones in order to become worthy recipients of divine love.

The problem becomes even more complicated if one consults the works of the Muslim theologians. For a major strand of Muslim theology has difficulty with ascribing love to God, even if He describes Himself as *al-Wadūd* in the Qur'ān. Such theological schools as the Jahmiyya,[6] the Mu'tazila, and the dominant school of *kalām* in Islam, the Ash'ariyya, identified God's 'love' with His will. For example, the Mu'tazilite Abū 'Alī al-Jubbā'ī (d. 303/915), in common with the rest of his school, sees a near-equivalence between God's love and His will (*irāda*): God's love for His creatures is only an expression of His will to reward and honour them in the Hereafter.[7] Abū Ḥasan al-Ash'arī

[6] According to Ibn Taymiyya, it was the teacher of al-Jahm b. Ṣafwān (d.128/745-6), al-Ja'd b. Dirham (d. 105/723-4), who is regarded as the first theologian to deny that God loves His creatures. See his *Kitāb majmū'at fatāwā* (Cairo: Maṭba'at Kurdistān al-'Ilmiyya, 1326-1329/1908-1911), vol. 1, pp.207-208. Cited by Joseph N. Bell, *Love Theory in Later Ḥanbalite Islam* (Albany: State University of New York, 1979), p.60 and p.233, n.93.

[7] Daniel Gimaret, *Les Noms divins en Islam* (Paris: Les Editions du Cerf, 1988),

(d. 324/935), erstwhile disciple and then opponent of al-Jubbāʾī, and founder of the most influential school of theology in Islam, is largely at one with his former teacher in regard to the meaning of God's love; he states that, in addition to willing or desiring to reward His creatures in the Hereafter, God's 'love' also consists in willing them to be believers—even though He knows from all eternity who will be and who will not be a believer.[8] For al-Ashʿarī, God's compassion (*raḥma*), His approval (*riḍā*) and His love are alike aspects of His beneficent will (*irādat al-inʿām*). He differs from the Muʿtazilites, however, in his occasional references to these attributes of God as being *identical* with His will, and not just aspects or forms assumed by His will. Thus, for al-Ashʿarī, everything that God wills is also, by definition, 'loved' and 'approved' by Him, including even bad actions: one has to define, however, the precise manner in which His love and approval are exercised.[9]

Despite this reservation, al-Ashʿarī's doctrine led to such impasses as the following : if God wills everything, and thus loves everything, how can the Qurʾān describe Him in good logic as not loving those things willed by Him, such as the immoral acts of the disbelievers? Although, as will be seen below, the gnosis of the Sufis as a whole transcended this volitive perspective on God, within the realm of theology, it fell to the neo-Ḥanbalite school to rectify this inordinate and massive stress on the will by the Ashʿarites. The equivalence between will and love was strongly opposed within the domain of scholastic theology by, for example, Ibn Taymiyya who asserted not only that God's love is real, and is not reducible to His will, but also that this will itself presupposed love: 'Every will necessarily requires a love, for everything willed is willed only because it is loved or because it is a means to something loved. If love is assumed not to exist, then will is an impossibility.'[10]

Another immensely influential Ashʿarite theologian al-Bāqillānī (d.404/1013) asserts forcefully that such emotional qualities as love

pp.424-425.

8 Ibid., p.425

9 See Daniel Gimaret, *La Doctrine d'al-Ashʿarī* (Paris: Les Éditions du Cerf, 1990), p. 195.

10 Bell, *Love Theory*, p.65. One should also note that there were Sufis who upheld Ashʿarism on the theological plane while transcending its precepts on the plane of gnosis (*maʿrifa*)—despite his critique of theology generally, al-Ghazzālī himself is still referred to as 'an Ashʿarite theologian'.

and anger can only be ascribed to God as indications of divine recompense for good and evil, respectively. Divine love can only mean 'God's will to reward those with whom He is satisfied, whom He loves and befriends'; and His anger means simply His will 'to punish those with whom He is angered, whom He hates and to whom He shows enmity. Nothing else!' If one tries to define love and anger in terms of anything other than His will to do good or harm, then one will fall into anthropomorphism: one will be ascribing to God 'an aversion and a change arising in His nature when He is angered, and a tenderness, inclination and tranquility in His nature when He is pleased'—which is impossible for God.[11]

In the following generation, another Ashᶜarite, al-Juwaynī (d. 478/1085) (the teacher of al-Ghazzālī), denies that God's love implies any of the humanly recognizable features of love such as sympathy, passion and need for fulfillment in another; to say that God loves a person is simply a way of saying that he grants that person favour and grace. He goes further than his predecessors in asserting that since love and will are identical, and since will can only be exercised over an object occurring in time, it follows that God, who has no beginning or end in time, cannot be the object of man's will, hence He cannot be the object of man's love.[12]

As is evident, the theologians of Islam exercise extreme caution when speaking about love in relation to God. This is because of their acute need to stress above all else the aspect of transcendence or incomparability (*tanzīh*) of God. This stress on divine transcendence, in turn, is based on the definitive credal principle of *tawḥīd*, the affirmation of divine unity. For God's uniqueness (that is, the transcendent one-and-onliness of ultimate reality) strictly requires a denial of any comparability between Him and His creation: 'There is nothing like Him' (42:11). If there were anything comparable to Him, then that 'thing' would undermine the absolute uniqueness of God, it would be a 'partner' with God: and to ascribe a partner to God constitutes the cardinal sin in Islam, that of *shirk*: idolatry, polytheism. If no thing is like Him, it follows that He is not like any thing: any attribution

[11] Bell, *Love Theory*, p.56.

[12] 'For a willer may only will that something exist which does not already exist and which can exist, or that something not cease to exist which can cease to exist. But that which is established as preeternal and insusceptible to nonexistence cannot be the object of will'. Cited in Ibid., p.59.

to God of a quality, such as love, which appears to bring Him into a mode of comparability with His creatures blurs this fundamental distinction between the Absolute and the relative, and thus is seen by the theologian as undermining the principle of *tawḥīd*. Most theologians, then, find themselves compelled to engage in a kind of implicit or explicit reductionism in relation to the divine name and attribute, 'The Loving', to ensure that divine 'love' had nothing in common with what is normally understood as love on the human plane. If love is described in humanly familiar terms as a kind of longing (*taḥannun*) or a passionate desire (*ᶜishq*) or even as an inclination (*mayl*), seeking a consummation as yet unrealised, then, on several theological counts, it cannot be ascribed to God: where and how and can such a love be ascribed to a transcendent Reality which possesses absolute unicity, infinite perfection, utter immutability and eternal synchronicity? Absolute unicity means there is no peer or like or partner or consort that God could love; infinite perfection means that there can be no state or quality lacking in God that He might lovingly aspire to realize; utter immutability means that God cannot in any sense be said to undergo change, moving from one state to another, such as is presupposed by love; eternal synchronicity means that whatever God is now, He has always been and will always be, and this precludes any possibility of attaining, through love, an object as yet unattained. In short, to quote al-Juwaynī: 'The Lord utterly transcends everything which indicates temporal contingency or deficiency.'[13]

Against this theological background it is not hard to see why many in the West arrived at the caricature described in the introduction to this article. Whereas the principle 'God is Love' is at the core of Christian theology, this principle, it is argued, is either non-existent in Islam or else derivative, having been borrowed apologetically from Christianity, whose very essence is defined in terms of the overflowing love of God: 'For God so loved the world, that He gave His only-begotten Son, that whosoever believeth in him should not perish, but have everlasting life.' (John, 3:16)

Given this *a priori* Christian conception of divine love in terms of a fatherly love for the creation, on the one hand, and given the centrality of scholastic theology within Christian thought on the other,

[13] *Kitāb al-lumaᶜ fī qawāᶜid Ahl al-Sunna*, in Michel Allard, *Textes apologétiques de Ğuwainī—Textes arabes traduits et annotés* (Beirut: Dar el-Machreq, 1968), p. 149.

it was altogether natural for early Christian investigation of Islam to focus firstly on Islamic theology, and secondly to look for something analogous to the Christian conception of a loving God within that theology, on the other. This initial orientation pre-determined the ensuing stereotype: for, as seen above, Muslim theologians, far from describing God in terms of love, debated the very legitimacy of ascribing love to God in any essential manner. But this is only one side of the story, a fragment of a discourse and a fraction of a universe vibrant with divine love, a universe in which God's love for creation constitutes both the context and the content of one's life and thought as a spiritually sensitive Muslim. Moving from a narrow theological view of divine love to a broader spiritual perspective helps us to debunk the stereotype of a love-less God in Islam.

2. From Theology to Spirituality

To debunk the stereotype, then, it should be clearly stated, first of all, that theology—*kalām*—does not play anything like the determinative role within Islam as it does within Christianity. The inner life and spiritual sensibility of the Muslim is not determined by theological doctrines, to say the least. The great 'renewer' (*mujaddid*) of Islam, al-Ghazzālī (d.1111), puts the case very forcefully in his 'Book of Knowledge', volume one of his magisterial and immensely influential *Iḥyāʾ ʿulūm al-dīn* ('Enlivening the sciences of religion'): the theologian, *al-mutakallim*, knows only the outward aspects of the creed (*al-ʿaqīda*), and these pertain to the external aspects of the heart and of speech. As regards knowledge (*maʿrifa*) of God, His qualities and His acts, one must know that 'this spiritual knowledge cannot be attained by the science of theology (*lā yuḥṣal min ʿilm al-kalām*)'. Rather, he asserts, theology is almost like 'a veil' (*ḥijāb*) obscuring this knowledge, and 'a barrier' (*māniʿ*) against it. The sole means of attaining true knowledge of God and His qualities is through the grace of luminous guidance granted by God, a grace described as being preceded by another grace, that of spiritual discipline, struggle against the faults of one's soul—*mujāhada*. 'The only way to attain this knowledge is through spiritual struggle, which God has established as the prelude to Guidance' (*innamā 'l-wuṣūl ilayhi bi 'l-mujāhada allatī ja'alahā 'Llāhu subhānahu muqaddiman li 'l-hidāya*).[14] The subtlety

[14] *Iḥyāʾ ʿulūm al-dīn* (Beirut: Dār al-Jīl, 1992), p.34; see the English translation

of the wording here is to be noted: it is divine guidance, alone, which bestows the knowledge in question, and this is preceded—but not produced or caused—by the acts of the seeker, those acts being necessary but not sufficient conditions for the guidance; necessary for the purification of the seeker, but insufficient in relation to grace of the Sought. Moreover, the spiritual discipline, itself, is seen as a grace by means of which effective action can be accomplished for the sake of the attainment of knowledge of God and His qualities and actions.

Thus, in order to appreciate the deepest meaning of the nature of divine reality within the Islamic universe of discourse, and to arrive at a more profound understanding of the meaning of God as 'the Loving', it is not to the theologians that one should look in the first instance, but rather, to those who made this spiritual struggle, *mujāhada*, the foundation of their lives; and this means focusing on the works of the Sufis. One of the key premises of this paper is that the spiritual perspectives of the Sufis had, and to some extent still have, a much greater resonance with grass-roots Muslims than do the abstruse concepts of the theologians or the legalistic precepts of the jurists. So when we turn our attention to the mystics of Islam, we should not think that we are departing from the mainstream of Muslim society; rather, the Sufis raised to their highest pitch, and plumbed to their deepest implications, the mostly unarticulated spiritual impulses of the masses; and their influence over the whole of society—in terms of arts, crafts, literature, and the sciences, from one end of the Muslim world to the other—cannot be fully accounted for in the absence of this spiritually 'leavening' role. Marshall Hodgson, one of the most sensitive observers of Islam as an integrated civilisation, was acutely aware of this:

> 'Sufism ...became the framework within which all popular piety flowed together; its saints, dead and living, became the guarantors of the gentle and co-operative sides of social life. Guilds commonly came to have Sufi affiliations. Men's clubs claimed the patronage of Sufi saints.[15] And the tombs of lo-

of Nabih Amin Faris, *The Book of Knowledge* (Lahore: Sh. Muhammad Ashraf), 1970 (rpr), p.55, which we have not followed. Also to be noted here is the following: 'All that theology offers in the way of useful evidence is contained in the Qur'ān and Hadith. Whatever evidence is not contained therein is either reprehensible argumentation, or mere wrangling over distinctions set up by opposing sects ...'. *Iḥyā'*, p.33 (Faris tr., p.53).

15 This Sufi affiliation was not exclusive to men: in medieval Islam it was by no

cal saints became shrines which almost all factions united in revering. It is probable that without the subtle leaven of the Sufi orders, giving to Islam an inward personal thrust and to the Muslim community a sense of participation in a common spiritual venture quite apart from anyone's outward power, the mechanical arrangements of the Shari'ah would not have maintained the loyalty essential to their effectiveness.'[16]

Thus, if we wish to appreciate the meaning of God's love within Islam, Sufi doctrines and perspectives can be investigated without fear of drifting from the moorings of Islamic society. To speak of the doctrines of the Sufis is to speak about the deepest spiritual values of the Islamic revelation—the Qur'ān and the Sunna—not about some extraneous and luxuriant speculations of a mystical minority isolated from the wider community of Muslims. On the contrary, it is precisely because of their fidelity to the spiritual values of the revelation that the Sufis were able to resonate so deeply with the aspirations and the sensibilities of ordinary Muslims. It would not be out of place to support this contention by citing the following anecdote from a recent important work by Seyyed Hossein Nasr. After making a pilgrimage to the shrine of the Sufi saint, Mian Mir, on the outskirts of Lahore in the 1960s, he recalls taking a horse-drawn carriage (a *tonga*) back to the city. It was driven by a poor, scantily-dressed man who, upon discovering that his passenger was Persian, began reciting line after line of Sufi poetry from Rūmī, Ḥāfiẓ and ᶜAṭṭār: 'That example—riding in the carriage that night under the starry sky of the Punjabi countryside listening to an illiterate *tonga* driver reciting some of the most sublime mystical love poetry ever written, reciting both from memory and from the center of his heart—shows how universal the living reality of the love for God is in the Islamic spiritual universe.' He then adds this important point: 'This love uses the sublime language of the Sufi poets, but this poetry speaks for all those Muslims, technically Sufi and non-Sufi alike, who are aware of God's love for

means uncommon to find Sufi lodges founded by women for the sake of women. The cities of Aleppo, Cairo and Baghdad were notable in this regard. For example, in Aleppo alone, between 1150 and 1250 no less than 7 female *khāniqahs* (Sufi lodges) were established. See J. Spencer Trimingham and John Voll, *The Sufi Orders in Islam* (Oxford: OUP, 1998) p.18.

16 Marshall G.H. Hodgson, *The Venture of Islam—Conscience and History in a World Civilization* (Chicago and London: Chicago University Press, 1974), vol. II, 'The Expansion of Islam in the Middle Periods', p.125.

His creation ...'[17]

It is important to stress here that the Sufis saw themselves—and still see themselves today—as doing nothing other than perpetuating the spiritual dimension of the legacy which they inherited from their predecessors, going all the way back to the Prophet and his companions. This is made clear in one of the most revealing definitions of Sufism, given by an authoritative Sufi himself, ᶜAlī al-Hujwīrī (d.1063): 'Today, Sufism is a name without a reality; formerly [i.e., in the Prophet's time] it was a reality without a name.'[18]

Nonetheless, there still remains the suspicion in western academic circles that the Sufis may not be altogether representative of the specifically Islamic revelation; theories still abound that the mystical doctrines of the Sufis originated in various Christian or Buddhist or Hindu influences. Nowadays this suspicion is being dispelled by scholars who have, following Massignon,[19] shown the Qurᵓānic roots of the central concepts employed by the Sufis in the elaboration of their mystical perspectives.

When we turn to the Sufis we are overwhelmed by the sheer exuberance of their proclamation of love, human and divine. Love for the Sufis is at the very heart of being, the whole cosmos vibrates and pulsates with that love which eternally flows from the very heart of God. Many books could be filled with this kind of 'love mysticism' expressed by the Sufis. It suffices for our purposes here to give a few brief 'tastes' of this view of Gods' love, using passages from two great Sufis, Rūmī and Ibn ᶜArabī, by way of illustration of this rich vein of Islamic spirituality.[20]

[17] Seyyed Hossein Nasr, *The Heart of Islam—Enduring Values for Humanity* (New York: HarperCollins, 2002), p.215.

[18] *The Kashf al-Maḥjūb—The Oldest Persian Treatise on Sufiism*, ᶜAlī al-Hujwīrī (tr. R.A Nicholson), (Lahore, Islamic Book Service, 1992), p. 44.

[19] See his pioneering work, *Essai sur les origins du lexique technique de la mystique musulmane* (Paris : Librairie Philosophique J. Vrin, 1968). For a view of this theme from within the Sufi tradition, see Martin Lings, *What is Sufism?* (Cambridge: Islamic Texts Society, 1993), and Abū Bakr Sirāj ad-Dīn *The Book of Certainty* (Cambridge: Islamic Texts Society, 1992), both of which are excellent works disclosing the extent to which the essence of Sufism is rooted in the Qur'ān; see also M. Lings 'The Nature and Origin of Sufism' (pp.223-238) and S.H. Nasr 'The Quran as the Foundation of Islamic Spirituality' (pp.3-10) in S.H. Nasr (ed) *Islamic Spirituality*, vol. 1 'Foundations' (London: Routledge & Kegan Paul, 1987).

[20] See Seyyed Hossein Nasr, *The Heart of Islam—Enduring Values for Humanity* (New York: HarperCollins, 2002) ch.5 'Compassion and Love, Peace and Beauty',

Jalāl al-Dīn Rūmī

In one simple line of his Mathnawī,[21] Rūmī addresses and transcends the theological reservation about speaking of God in terms of love: 'Love is one of the attributes of that divine reality which needs nothing'.[22] God has no need of anything, and yet love is indeed one of His attributes, and not just love in the sense connoted by the divine name al-Wadūd or even al-Muḥibb, but love in the passionate sense implied in *ᶜishq*, the word Rūmī uses in this line. While *wudd* or *ḥubb* might be tolerated by the theologian as a quality of God, the ascription of *ᶜishq* to God was severely censured, as this most emphatically appeared to endow God with a need, the need of the passionate lover for the beloved. Rūmī thus seems to be deliberately and provocatively juxtaposing the two elements, the theological concept of a God beyond all need, and an ascription to God of, not just love, but a passionate love. It is as if, in this single line, he is calling out for a spiritual act of recognition of two apparently contradictory notions, and the intellect is unable to reconcile the two, for:

> 'Whatever I say in exposition and explanation of love, when I come to Love itself, I am ashamed of all that... In expounding it [love], the intellect lay down [helplessly], like an ass in the mire; it was Love alone that uttered the

pp.201-236, for a succinct presentation of these fundamental themes in the Islamic tradition; Gai Eaton, *Islam and the Destiny of Man* (Albany, NY: Islamic Texts Society/George Allen & Unwin, 1985), chapter entitled 'Truth and Mercy', pp.52-69 for a profound and eloquent exposition of these two dominant motifs in Islamic spirituality; Annemarie Schimmel, *Mystical Dimensions of Islam* (Chapel Hill, NC: University of North Carolina Press, 1975), for a comprehensive overview of mystical traditions within Islam, with a particular accentuation on the theme of love within Sufism; Margaret Smith, *Rabi'a the Mystic and Her Fellow Saints in Islam* (Cambridge: Cambridge University Press, 1928) for an account of the doctrines of the great female saint, Rābiᶜa al-ᶜAdawiyya, often described as the pioneer of love-mysticism in Islam. The early development of this love-oriented mysticism is well presented in the essay by Carl Ernst 'The Stages of Love in Early Persian Sufism, from Rābiᶜa to Rūzbihān', in Leonard Lewisohn (ed.) *The Heritage of Sufism*, vol.1, 'Classical Persian Sufism from its origins to Rumi (700—1300)' (Oxford: Oneworld, 1999), pp.435-455.

21 The *Mathnawī* is often referred to in Persia as a poetic commentary on the Qurʾān. Indeed, as Corbin notes, it is 'meditated and practised as the "Persian Qurʾān" (*Qurʾān-i Fārsī*)'. *En Islam iranien* (Paris: Gallimard, 1971), vol. III, pp. 216-217.

22 *Mathnawī-i maᶜnawī* (Tehran: Bihzād, 1371 Sh.), book 6, line 974, p.965; See Nicholson's translation, *The Mathnawi of Jalaladdin Rumi* (London: Luzac, 1934), book 6, line 971, p. 312, which we have not followed.

explanation of love and loverhood.'[23]

It is only by means of love that divine love can be understood, love being 'the astrolabe of the mysteries of God'.[24] One needs to plumb the depths of love within one's own heart in order to understand the love that God is by His deepest nature; here, Rūmī is but poetically expressing a key Qur°ānic principle: 'We shall show them Our signs on the horizons and in their own souls, until it be clear to them that He is the Real' (Fuṣṣilat, 41:53) The word for 'signs' is the same as the word for verses of the revelation, *āyāt* (sing. *āya*), and the implication here is that the revelation of God's reality is given not just by the verses of scripture, but also by that outward revelation of His nature which the whole cosmos is, and that inward revelation constituted by intellectual apprehension and contemplative assimilation. Rūmī's lines here express the need to gauge the divine mysteries by means of the 'astrolabe' of love, for love alone deciphers the signs and reveals its own divine essence: 'The proof of the sun is the sun'.[25]

Ibn ᶜArabī

The 12th century Spanish mystic, Muḥyiddīn Ibn al-ᶜArabī is known by the epithet of 'the Greatest Master' (al-Shaykh al-Akbar), on account of the sheer scope and depth of the doctrines expounded by him, and the influence of these doctrines on the subsequent development of Sufism. Love is described by him as the very principle or root (*aṣl*) of Being (*kitāb al-maḥabba*). He writes in his most commented work, *Fuṣūṣ al-ḥikam*: 'That movement constituted by the very being of the cosmos is a movement of love (*al-ḥaraka allatī hiya wujūd al-ᶜālam ḥarakatu ḥubbin*).'[26] It is not just that everything which occurs in life is a cosmic dance of love: the very process by which being emerges from non-being is described by Ibn al-ᶜArabī as a movement initiated, sustained and consummated by God's love. In common with many Sufis he cites the famous *ḥadīth qudsī* or 'divine saying', transmitted by the Prophet: 'I was a hidden treasure and I loved to be

[23] Ibid, Book 1, line 115; (identical reference in *Mathnawī*, Persian original)

[24] Ibid, Book 1, line 110.

[25] Ibid, Book 1, line 116.

[26] *Fuṣūṣ al-ḥikam* (Cairo: al-Maṭbaᶜa al-Maymaniyya, 1321/1903), p.256. See the translation by Caner Dagli, *The Ringstones of Wisdom* (Chicago: Kazi Publications, 2004), p.261, which I have not followed.

known, so I created the creation in order to be known',[27] and adds: 'If it were not for this love, the world would never have appeared in this concrete existence. In this sense, the movement of the world from nonexistence toward existence was a movement of Love.'[28]

In Ibn ᶜArabī's complex cosmogony, the love of God to be known is linked with the mercy of God in the most surprising manner: for God has 'mercy' upon His own names and qualities which are yearning to be known in outward existence. God's love to be known stems from that aspect of the divine reality or 'treasure' which wishes to manifest its properties. So, however contradictory it may sound, God has mercy upon Himself, 'breathing' upon His own names and qualities thus bringing them into existence through loving compassion. The 'breath of the Compassionate' (*nafas al-Raḥmān*) is the existentiating force behind the cosmos in its entirety:

> 'Do you not see how the Absolute breathed out and relieved the Divine Names of (the pain of compression) which they had been feeling because of the non-appearance of their effects, in an entity called the world? This happened because the Absolute loves relaxation (*rāḥa*). And relaxation was only to be obtained through the existence of forms. Thus is it patent that movement is caused by love, and that there can be no movement in the world but that it is motivated by Love.'[29]

[27] This saying is one of the cornerstones of Sufi metaphysics. However, it is not regarded by scholars of Ḥadīth as having an authentic chain of transmission, though the same scholars accept its meaning and message, by reference to the verse 'And We only created the jinn and mankind in order that they might worship Me', and to the comment on this by Ibn ᶜAbbās: the phrase 'that they might worship Me' means 'that they might know Me'.

[28] Fuṣūṣ, p.256; Cf. Dagli trans., pp.261-2.

[29] Fus. 256. It is interesting to note that Ibn Sīnā—and following him, most of the Muslim philosophers—had a similar vision of an *ᶜishq* which is at one with the very nature of being, penetrating and directing all existents. God's wisdom and governance 'plant into everything the general principle of love'; and, since 'the good is loved in its very essence', on the one hand, and since God is the supreme good, on the other, it follows that all things love and tend towards God as the supreme object of love. Ibn Sīnā also defines the divine Essence in terms of love: 'The highest subject of love is identical with the highest object of love, namely Its [God's] high and sublime Essence … And because there is no distinction among the divine qualities of Its Essence, love is here the Essence and Being purely and simply … In all beings, therefore, love is either the cause of their being, or being and love are identical with them.' See E.L. Fackenheim's translation of Ibn Sīnā's *Risāla fī'l-ᶜishq*, 'A Treatise on Love by Ibn Sīnā', in *Mediaeval Studies*, 7 (1945), pp. 213-214.

Divine love is thus inseparable from divine mercy, and both are inseparable from the very substance of the universe:

> 'His breathing is a property of the Love by which He described Himself in the saying, 'I loved to be known' ... Hence this Divine Breathing is identical with the existence of the cosmos ... so the cosmos is identical with mercy, nothing else.'[30]

This stress on the inseparability of love and mercy within the divine nature and thus within this world, which is nothing but the manifestation of that nature 'loving to be known', leads us back to the Qur'ān. For Ibn ʿArabī's perspective, in spite of its complex metaphysical elaborations, arises organically out of the spiritual principle of loving mercy or compassionate love which is inscribed in the heart of the Qur'ānic revelation.

3. Revelation Revisited: *Raḥma* as all-encompassing Love

Many might be of the opinion that the exalted view of divine love expressed by such mystics has little if anything to do with the Qur'ān.[31] But, as mentioned above, this is contradicted by the mystics themselves, who assert that whatever inspiration they may have received is but the fruit of their assimilation of the message of the Qur'ān and the Prophet. Ibn ʿArabī cites this saying of Abū Madyan (d. 1198), the seminal Maghribi spiritual authority from whom many Sufi orders claim descent: 'The spiritual aspirant (*al-murīd*) is not a true aspirant until he finds in the Qur'ān everything to which he aspires.'[32]

We might go further and say that, as regards divine love, it is not just the Sufis but every sensitive Muslim who concretely feels the all-embracing love of God, this, in the very measure of their receptivity

[30] W.C. Chittick, *The Sufi Path of Knowledge* (Albany: State University of New York Press, 1989), p.131, citing *al-Futūḥāt*, vol.II p.437, line 20.

[31] B. Abrahamov, surveys the theme of love in the Qur'ān and *Ḥadīth* in less than two pages and concludes: 'It is obvious that such scanty material, at least concerning the plain meaning of the Qur'anic verses, could not be the source of the great theories of divine love which were developed later in Islam.' Binyamin Abrahamov, *Divine Love in Islamic Mysticism—The Teachings of Al-Ghazali and Al-Dabbagh* (London/New York: RoutledgeCurzon, 2003), p.14.

[32] Ibn al-ʿArabī, *al-Futūḥāt al-Makkiyya* (Cairo, 1329 AH), vol. 3, p.94, line 2. Cited by Michel Chodkiewicz, *Un océan sans rivage—Ibn Arabî, le livre et le loi* (Paris : Éditions du Seuil, 1992), p.47. In this same passage, Ibn al-ʿArabī asserts that when the Qur'ān truly 'descends' upon the heart, and not just the tongue, the result is a sweetness (*ḥalāwa*) beyond all measure, surpassing all delight (*ladhdha*).

to the spiritual substance of the Qurʾānic revelation. This love may be indefinable in its ultimate essence but it is undeniable as regards its penetrating presence; it is evasive conceptually, but all-pervasive existentially. Disclosed by everything beautiful, yet enclosed by nothing; expressed by every loving subject and lovable object, yet exhausted by none. This is so because the Muslim does not view God's love only through the prism of the divine Name *al-Wadūd*, nor, still less, through the spectacles of theology; rather, the love of God is perceived and received as an all-embracing quality of creative being, and not simply conceived as an anthropomorphic emotion writ large and superimposed on God.

Divine love is seen and felt as a quality streaming forth in innumerable outpourings of the divine spirit—in the form of the beauty of virgin nature, in the beauty and wisdom of divine guidance through the scriptures and through heavenly messengers, in the sanctity of the saints, indeed, in every conceivable and perceivable form of love, goodness, beauty and beatitude that can be found around us and within us, surging up from the primordial, God-given nature of the human soul, the *fiṭra*: 'We shall show them Our signs on the horizons and in their own souls so that it be clear to them that He is the Real.' (41:53)

These outpourings of the spirit of love are designated, and at the deepest level, constituted,[33] by the names and attributes and acts of God. Just as, on the human plane, love assumes several forms—conjugal love, filial love, parental love, sibling love, etc.—while being reducible to none of them, so, *a fortiori*, divine love assumes a panoply of self-manifestations, while being reducible to none of them. A dazzling configuration of divine qualities is summoned up before the Muslim devotee when reading the Qurʾān, qualities which are infused with love, radiate love and generate love. In addition to *al-Wadūd*, we have such names as *al-Raḥmān*, the lovingly Compassionate, *al-Raḥīm*, the lovingly Merciful, *al-Laṭīf*, the Loving-Kind, *al-Walī*, the loving Friend, *al-Karīm*, the Generous, *al-Barr*, the Benevolent, *al-Ḥalīm*, the Gentle, *al-Raʾūf*, the Kind, *al-Wakīl*, the Absolutely Trustworthy, *al-Ghafūr*, the Forgiver, *al-ʿAfū*, the Effacer of Sin, *al-Tawwāb*, the Relenting, and so on. Each of these qualities is

[33] 'By Thy Names, which have filled the foundations of all things', as Imam ʿAlī says in his famous supplication entitled *Duʿāʾ Kumayl*, in *Supplications: Amīr al-Muʾminīn*, tr. W.C. Chittick (London: Muhammadi Trust, 1995), verse 4.

felt to be a manifestation of love according to a particular modality; the totality of these names and qualities—and the acts which manifest them—bestows not just a sense of the effusion of love from God to creation, but also, in their very diversity, this configuration of qualities expresses something of the infinite and thus ultimately transcendent essence of God's love. This love both penetrates and reintegrates the whole of creation, a reintegration or 'making one'—the essence of *tawḥīd*—with the One, whose very infinitude defies definition, hence the love in question is both inescapable in its manifestations, and ungraspable in its essence: immanent and transcendent.

In addition to these specific divine Names, we have a whole set of acts and descriptions which express loving qualities, but from which divine names in the theological sense, are not classically derived:

> 'He is of tremendous bounty' (*Huwa dhu'l-faḍl al-ʿaẓīm*) we are told repeatedly in the Qurʾān.
>
> 'Every single good thing you have is [a grace] from God' (16:53).
>
> God's graces are boundless, and thus innumerable: 'Were you to count the graces of God, you could not number them' (14:34).[34]
>
> His gracious gifts (*ʿaṭāʾ*) are showered both upon those who reject Him and those who strive for Him: 'Unto each, the former and the latter, do We extend the gracious gift of thy Lord. And the gracious gift of thy Lord can never be confined behind walls (*maḥẓūra*)' (17:20).
>
> 'Do you not see how God hath made serviceable to you whatever is in the skies and on earth, and has lavished His blessings upon you, both outwardly and inwardly?' (31:20)

All of these descriptions of God's acts and attributes and nature are brought together in a myriad of combinations, associations and implications, and are apprehended by the Muslim as so many mutually illuminating stars in a veritable constellation of divine love: 'Light upon light', *nūr ʿalā nūr*, as the Qurʾān says in one of its most graphic symbols of the divine mystery, telling us that God is the Light of the

[34] Note the gifts of creation in the two verses preceding this verse.

Heavens and the earth.[35]

The question will of course be raised: What of the opposite kind of names of qualities, those of anger, wrath, chastisement, and so on? These are certainly found and found in abundance in the Qurʾān, but they cannot alter the conception of God as primarily, overwhelmingly, inherently, and essentially loving. It is of the utmost importance to understand that this constellation of loving qualities (referred to in terms of *luṭf*, loving-kindness or *jamāl*, beauty) is viewed as being much more indicative of the core of the divine nature—closer to the 'pole' of ultimate reality—than is the constellation of wrathful qualities (pertaining to *qahr*, all-conquering power, or *jalāl*, majesty). For these rigorous qualities are to be seen in the light of the loving qualities, which brilliantly overshadow them. What are the bases of this assertion?

As regards the Qurʾānic basis for the assertion that God is inherently and overwhelmingly loving, one should focus first of all upon the two names of mercy: *al-Raḥmān* and *al-Raḥīm*.[36] Every chapter of the Qurʾān except one begins with the phrase: *Bismi 'Llāh al-Raḥmān al-Raḥīm*, which could be translated as: In the Name of God, the lovingly Compassionate, the lovingly Merciful, for the quality expressed by both of these names of mercy is *raḥma*, and this quality is understood as combining both mercy and love. In other words, the word is close to the meaning of *caritas* in Latin and *agape* in Greek, and can be translated as 'charity' in the strictly etymological sense of the word, and not in the reduced sense that has become conventional today.[37] Just as love is the inherent, defining reality of charity, so *raḥma* is

[35] For Sufi commentaries on the famous 'verse of light' (24:35) see Kristin Zahra Sands, *Ṣūfī Commentaries on the Qurʾān in Classical Islam* (London & New York: Routledge, 2006), pp.110-135.

[36] It is to be noted that al-Ghazzālī, in his commentary on the divine names, refers to *al-Wadūd* as being close in meaning to *al-Raḥīm*, but whereas the latter requires an object in need of mercy, *al-Wadūd* bestows its graces from the outset upon all, not requiring any such object, this being among the consequences of the quality of love (*al-inʿām ʿalā sabīl al-ibtidāʾ min natāʾij al-wudd*). See his *The Ninety-Nine Beautiful Names of God (al-Maqṣad al-asnā fī sharḥ asmāʾ Allāh al-ḥusnā)* (tr. D.B. Burrell, N. Daher) (Cambridge: Islamic Texts Society, 1999), p.119. Al-Ghazālī, *Al-Maqṣad al-asnā fī sharḥ asmāʾ Allāh al-ḥusnā* (Arabic text), ed. Fadlou A. Shehadi (Beirut: Dar El-Machreq, 1971) p.132.

[37] The King James translation of *caritas/agape* as 'charity', in the moving letter of St Paul to the Corinthians, where charity is described as greater than hope and faith, is quite correct, since the primary meaning of the word, even according to the Oxford English Dictionary today, is love.

to be understood primarily in terms of a love which gives of itself: what it gives is what it is, transcendent beatitude, which creates out of love, and, upon contact with Its creation, assumes the nature of loving compassion and mercy, and the whole myriad of qualities mentioned earlier. As will be seen in a saying of the Prophet below, God's transcendent *raḥma* is alluded to in terms of the most striking expression of *raḥma* on earth—that expressed by a mother who, after searching frantically for her baby, clutches it to her breast and feeds it: 'God is more merciful to His servants than is this woman to her child.' In English, one speaks of a mother's love for her child in such a context, rather than her mercy or compassion; thus, the quality of *raḥma* is far better translated into English as 'loving mercy' or 'merciful love', 'loving compassion' or 'compassionate love', than simply as 'mercy' or 'compassion'. The clear implication is that mercy/compassion flow forth from infinite love, and are inseparable from it.

The Jewish scholar Ben-Shemesh goes so far as to translate the *basmala* as 'In the Name of God, the Compassionate, the Beloved' to bring home this key aspect of love proper to the root of *raḥma*.[38] He argues that in both Arabic and Hebrew the meaning of love is strongly present in the root *r-ḥ-m*, and gives the following compelling evidence: Psalm number 18 contains the phrase: *Erḥamḥa Adonay*—'I love thee my Lord'.[39] In Aramaic/Syriac, the root *r-ḥ-m* specifically denotes love, rather than 'compassion'. One can thus feel the resonance of this Syriac connotation within the Arabic *raḥma*. Moreover, there is epigraphic evidence that early Christian sects in southern Arabic used the name *Raḥmānan* as a name of God, and this would probably have been understood as 'The Loving'.[40]

Raḥma, as loving compassion/compassionate love, is thus invoked in two forms at the very beginning of every chapter of the Qur᾿ān, and is the formula of consecration *par excellence* of Islam, uttered prior to initiating every important activity. It is recited 17 times each day, at least, by every practising Muslim in the canonical prayers. Al-Ghazzālī in his commentary on the divine Names, *al-Maqṣad al-asnā*, asserts

[38] See A. Ben Shemesh, 'Some Suggestions to Qur'an Translators', in *Arabica*, vol.16, no.1, 1969, p.82.

[39] Ibid.

[40] See Albert Jamme, 'Inscriptions on the Sabaean Bronze Horse of the Dumbarton Oaks Collection', in *Dumbarton Oaks Papers*, vol. 8 (1954), pp. 323-324 et passim.

that the name *al-Raḥmān* is close to the name *Allāh*, and cites the all-important verse: 'Call upon *Allāh* or call upon *al-Raḥmān*; whichever you call upon, unto Him belong the most beautiful names' (17:110). It should be noted in this verse that all the names are described as 'most beautiful', including therefore all the names of rigour as well as those of gentleness, this being another sign of the predominance of divine love and over divine anger.[41] But the most important point to note here is that the name *al-Raḥmān* is practically co-terminous with the name *Allāh*, indicating that the quality of loving mercy takes us to the very heart of the divine nature. Indeed, al-Ghazzālī explains the meaning of *al-Raḥmān* in terms of a loving inclination for he says: '[*al-Raḥmān*] is He who is lovingly inclined towards His creatures (*al-ᶜaṭūf ᶜalā 'l-ᶜibād*), first by creating them; second, by guiding them to faith and to the means of salvation; third by making them happy in the next world; and fourth by granting them contemplation of His noble Face.'[42] These principles are given considerable amplification in al-Ghazzālī's book on love (*kitāb al-maḥabba*) in his *Iḥyā'*, as will be seen below. But to remain with the name *al-Raḥmān* in Qur'ānic context, consider the following verses.

'He has prescribed mercy for Himself' (6: 12). The word *kataba*, 'he wrote', is used in this verse, so the literal meaning is: 'He wrote *raḥma* upon His own soul', implying that *raḥma* is a kind of inner law governing the very *nafs*, the Self or Essence of God. The use of the image of 'writing' here can be seen as a metaphor for expressing the metaphysical truth that *raḥma* is as it were 'inscribed' within the deepest reality of the divine nature. God's 'inscription' *upon* Himself is thus God's description *of* Himself. These considerations help us to see why the Names of love and mercy overshadow those of wrath and rigour within the divine nature.

In the chapter entitled '*al-Raḥmān*' (Sūra number 55), it is *al-Raḥmān* who 'taught the Qur'ān, created man, taught him discernment' (verses 1-3). The whole of this chapter evokes and invokes the real-

[41] It should be noted that in the central canonical prayer of the Qur'an, the *Fātiḥa*, it is mercy, compassion and lordship that are ascribed to God, and not anger, the penultimate verse *ghayri 'l-maghḍūbi ᶜalayhim*, 'not the path of those upon is anger', does not explicitly refer to God as the subject of anger. See our *My Mercy Encompasses All—The Koran's Teachings on Compassion, Peace and Love* (Emeryville, CA: Shoemaker and Hoard, 2007), pp.8-9.

[42] *The Ninety-Nine Beautiful Names*, p.54 (translation modified); Arabic text, p.66-67.

ity of this essential quality of God, at once creative and redemptive. Indisputably among the most sublime in the Qur'ān, its majestic meaning and magical musicality combine to produce a rhythm which sets in motion a transformative reverberation of creative love, a marvelously interiorizing melody which absorbs the contemplative soul of the reciter and directs its gaze towards the Paradises so irresistibly described.[43] The blessings of that Paradise are not restricted however to the next life, for the glories, beauties and harmonies of God's entire cosmos, including all the wonders of virgin nature, are also described in verses of supernal beauty, which are musically punctuated by the refrain: 'so which of the favours of your Lord can you deny?'. One of the 'favours' is, precisely, the revelation of such a beautiful invitation to contemplate the infinite 'favours', the graces both outward and inward, of the Lord. For, as already stressed above, there is no beauty, no harmony, no delight in the whole realm of creation that is not the grace or the favour of a loving Lord. In this chapter named after *al-Raḥmān*, then, we are invited to contemplate the various levels at which *raḥma* fashions the substance of reality: the *raḥma* that describes the deepest nature of the divine; the *raḥma* that is musically inscribed into the very recitation of the chapter; the *raḥma* that creates all things; the *raḥma* that reveals itself through the Qur'ān and through all the signs (*āyāt*) of nature. One comes to see that God has created not only *by raḥma*, and *from raḥma* but also *for raḥma*: '... except those upon whom God has mercy: for this did He create them' (11:119); and *within raḥma*: 'My *raḥma* encompasses all things' (7:156).

Al-Raḥmān is normally used to refer to the creative power of *raḥma*, and *al-Raḥīm*, to the salvific power of *raḥma*. Combining these two properties of loving compassion, the creative and redemptive, or the existential and salvational, we see why it is that ultimately nothing can escape or be separated from God's all-embracing *raḥma*.

Raḥma, then, is the divine matrix containing the cosmos, and the word 'matrix' should be taken quite literally, in relation to its root: 'mother'. The word for womb, *raḥim*, derives from the same root as

[43] For an illuminating exegesis of this sūra, and especially of the 'two paradises' mentioned therein, see Frithjof Schuon, 'The Two Paradises' in his *Form and Substance in the Religions* (Bloomington, IN: World Wisdom, 2002), pp.253-255. For Schuon's profound exposition of the message of the Qur'ān in general, see the chapter 'The Quran' in his *Understanding Islam* (Bloomington: World Wisdom, 1994), pp.39-94.

raḥma. The entire cosmos is not just brought into being by *raḥma*, it is perpetually encompassed by *raḥma* which nourishes it at every instant,[44] as the mother's womb nourishes and encompasses the embryo growing within it. The analogy evoked by this etymological relationship between maternal love and the compassionate matrix of creation is mysteriously implied in the chapter of the Qurʾān named after the Blessed Virgin, the Sūrat Maryam (chapter 19). For in this chapter we notice that the name *al-Raḥmān* is mentioned repeatedly as a virtual synonym for God: the Blessed Virgin seeks refuge in *al-Raḥmān* (19:18), she consecrates her fast to *al-Raḥmān* (19:26), Satan is described as the enemy of *al-Raḥmān* (19:44), when the verses revealed by *al-Raḥmān* are recited, the Prophets fall down prostrate (19:58), and so on. The name *al-Raḥmān* is repeated no less than 16 times—more times than in any other chapter of the Qurʾān.[45] Since this name occurs altogether 57 times in the sūras of the Qurʾān—that is, apart from its occurrence at the head of every sūra—this means that the Sūrat Maryam contains more than one quarter of all the instances in which the name *al-Raḥmān* comes in the Qurʾān.[46]

To conclude this part of the discussion: we have seen that calling upon Allāh is tantamount to calling upon *al-Raḥmān*, that all things are created by *raḥma*, for the sake of *raḥma*, and are encompassed by *raḥma*. This helps us to understand that God's *raḥma* is not just mercy but rather it is the infinite love and overflowing beatitude of ultimate reality, one of whose manifestations is mercy.

This still leaves the question unanswered: where is the place and what can be the role of the wrathful attributes of God? To answer this question, and to explore further the nature of divine love, we can turn to the sayings and to the soul of the Prophet.

The clearest possible articulation of the relationship between the qualities of love and those of anger is expressed in the well-attested saying of the Prophet, referring to what is inscribed on God's Throne:

[44] 'Every day, He performs a noble work' (*kulla yawmin huwa fī shaʾn*), according to the sūrat *al-Raḥmān*, 55:29.

[45] See the forthcoming set of interpretive essays by Samuel Tekin, *Christianity and Islam: Metaphysical Essays on Ontology, Archetype and the Perennial Philosophy* (London: Archetype/Matheson Trust, 2009), in which this remarkable feature of the chapter is also noted.

[46] The name *al-Raḥīm* occurs 95 times, apart from its occurrence in the *basmala*. The root, *r-ḥ-m* and its derivatives occurs 375 times, not including the 114 instances of the *basmala*.

'My mercy precedes My wrath'.[47] In Tirmidhī's collection, the word 'prevails' (*sabaqat*) is used: 'My mercy prevails over My wrath'.[48]

Mercy preceding or prevailing over wrath can be understood as an expression of the supereminence of love, and all associated qualities, which are deemed to be indicative of the essential nature of ultimate reality; the opposed qualities are to be seen as peripheral and accidental: their operation is to bring about a restoration of a ruptured equilibrium, so their goal is to bring things back to *raḥma*, and not to punish for the sake of inflicting pain. Love thus has a principial or ontological priority within the divine nature. Understanding this principle helps one to cast in a different light the following verses:

> 'And We have tied every man's augury to his own neck, and We shall bring forth for him on the Day of Judgement a book which he will find open wide. [It will be said to him:] Read your book. Your own soul suffices this day unto you as a reckoner.' (17:13)

> 'Whatever good comes to you is from God, and whatever evil comes to you is from your own soul' (4:79).

It is goodness, compassion, peace and love that emanate from God to man; whatever else man experiences is solely the result of his own deeds, attitudes and dispositions. It is not difficult to see why the mystics of Islam refer to God's 'anger' as being nothing but the extrinsic consequence of a lack of receptivity on the part of man to the mercy of God.[49] Divine wrath is seen here as contingent, not essential: contingent in the sense of being called forth by contingent action—human sin—and thereby defined in terms of a disequilibrium which must be rectified.

Let us return to the divine name, *al-Wadūd*, and consider two sayings of the Prophet which al-Ghazzālī cites as examples of the attitudes that conform to this divine name: 'The Messenger of God said, when his teeth were broken and his face was struck and bloodied:

[47] Bukhārī, *Ṣaḥīḥ*, II, *kitāb* (no. 63) *al-khalq*, *bāb* 1, *ḥadīth* no. 3022; Muslim, *Ṣaḥīḥ*, IV, *kitāb* (no. 49) *al-tawba*, *bāb* 4, *ḥadīth* no. 2751.

[48] Tirmidhī, *Sunan*, V, *bāb* no. 109, *ḥadīth* no. 3611.

[49] Fuṣūṣ, p.222, especially Kāshānī's comment, as noted and explored fully by Toshihiko Izutsu, *Sufism and Taoism—A Comparative Study of Key Philosophical Concepts* (Berkeley, Los Angeles, London, University of California Press, 1983), p.117 et passim.

'Lord, guide my people, for they do not know.'[50] The second one is this: He commanded ᶜAlī: 'If you want to precede the ones brought nigh, then be united with those who broke with you, give to the ones who excluded you, and forgive the ones who wronged you'.[51]

The theme of loving forgiveness of one's enemies is to be found concretely embodied in the Prophet's character and his actions. It is for this reason that we find him described in the Qur'ān as a *raḥma* to the whole of creation: 'We sent you not [O Prophet] save as a mercy for all the worlds.' (39:53)

> 'It was through the mercy of God that you [O Prophet] were gentle with them. For if you had been harsh and hard-hearted they would have fled from you. So pardon them, and pray that they be forgiven.' (3: 159)

The Prophet is described in terms of divine qualities, *ra'ūf, raḥīm*, kind and merciful:

> 'There hath come unto you a messenger from yourselves, for whom whatever burdens you is grievous to him, full of concern for you, kind and merciful to the believers.' (9:128)

The Prophet is named *al-Ḥabīb*, the beloved, or *Ḥabību'Llāh*, the beloved of God, and this means that he is the perfect model of a lovable human being: 'If you love God, follow me. God will love you' (3:31), as cited earlier; but now it should be clearer that following his example means ensuring that mercy, love and gentleness prevail within our souls, this being our way of mirroring the predominance of the same qualities within ultimate reality. It follows that entering into the mould of the prophetic love is to enter into the realm of the Real, and herein lies the fundamental aim of all prophecy. In the chapter entitled 'The Poets' (*al-Shuᶜarā'*, Sūra 26) we are given an allusion to this basic aim of all the prophets of God. After mentioning the stories of Moses, Abraham, Noah, Hūd, Ṣāliḥ, Lot, and Jethro, there is this refrain, as if it summed up the essence of the prophetic message: 'Truly thy Lord, He is indeed the gloriously Mighty, the lovingly Merciful (*al-ᶜAzīz, al-Raḥīm*)'. Here the combination of God's saving mercy, on the one hand, and His glorious inaccessibility, on the other, is stressed: the manifestation of love, and the eternally

[50] *Allāhumma'hdi qaumī fa-innahum lā yaᶜlamūn.*

[51] *Al-Maqṣad*, p.119.

unknowable essence of love.

A few concrete examples of the Prophet's teaching of the nature of divine love would be in order here. First, the context of the saying cited earlier in relation to the *raḥma* of the mother for her baby: Certain captives were brought to the Prophet. There was a woman among them, seen to be holding her breast and running after her baby; she found him, and held him to her breast and fed him. The Prophet said to his companions: 'Do you think this woman would cast her child into the fire?' We said, 'No, she could not do such a thing.' He said, 'God is more merciful to His servants than is this woman to her child.'[52]

Here the Prophet is affirming that the mercy of God is infinitely greater than the most intense form of mercy conceivable to human beings, that of the merciful love of the mother for her baby. At the same time, he taught that this kind of mercy can only exist by virtue of its prototype *in divinis*: it is because of God's loving mercy that this quality can be found among His creatures. This is affirmed in the following saying:

> 'On the Day He created the heavens and the earth, God created one hundred mercies, each mercy corresponding to the distance which is between the heavens and earth, and from these mercies He assigned one mercy on earth. It is by this mercy that His creatures are merciful towards one another, a mother will have affection for her child, and also birds and beasts towards one another.'[53]

Sayings of a similar import and nature can be multiplied indefinitely. The Prophet was described repeatedly in the earliest sources as *aḥlam al-nās*, the man most possessed of that quality of *ḥilm*, which is untranslatable by a single word in English. One needs to combine the following attributes to obtain some idea of the complexity of this virtue: gentleness (whence the divine name, *al-Ḥalīm*, the Gentle), wisdom, patience, kindness, self-control, calmness, and perhaps most of all, forbearance: that kind of forbearance which stems from knowledge of the consequences of actions and dispositions, and at the highest level, knowledge that forbearance in the human soul is attuned

[52] Bukhārī, *Ṣaḥīḥ*, *kitāb al-adab*, *bāb* 18 *ḥadīth* no. 5999 (Bukhari summarized: p.954, no.2015); Muslim, *Ṣaḥīḥ*, *kitāb al-tawba*, *ḥadīth* no. 6978.

[53] Bukhari summarized, p.954, no. 2015; Muslim, *Ṣaḥīḥ*, IV, *kitāb* (no. 49) *al-tawba*, *bāb* 4, *ḥadīth* no. 2753.

to the forbearance and mercy proper to the Omniscient Lord. The Prophet, whose knowledge of God was perfect, was a perfect mirror of the loving qualities which are inextricable from the consciousness that absolute reality has of itself: 'He has prescribed mercy for Himself', on the one hand; and He 'encompasses all things in mercy and knowledge' (40:7), on the other. To know God is to be at one with His mercy and His love.

4. Love and Union: *Walāya* and *Tawḥīd*

This takes our discussion to the more metaphysical aspects of divine love. As noted earlier, the *ḥadīth qudsī*, 'I was a hidden treasure, and I loved to be known, so I created the creation in order to be known', plays a role of fundamental importance in Islamic gnosis, that dimension of knowledge which is not abstract but concrete, not just posited discursively but 'realized' spiritually, that is, made 'real'; since ultimate reality is at one with love, 'realized' knowledge must be a perfect synthesis between the two principles, just as it must integrate knowledge within being. Without the dimension of love, knowledge remains abstract; realized knowledge is thus overflowing with love, and the consummation of love is beatific union with the Beloved, thus, *tawḥīd* in its deepest spiritual significance of 'making one'. Just as, according to the *ḥadīth qudsī*, love for being known initiates creation, so it is knowledge of God that brings about a love which consummates creation. In other words, it is consciousness of God that attracts the love of God, and this love reveals the ultimate meaning of the first testimony of Islam, 'No God but God'. It is this dimension of *tawḥīd* as union that the saints or the 'friends of God' (*awliyāʾ Allāh,* sing. *walī Allāh*) have realized.

In the following *ḥadīth qudsī*, to which the highest degree of authenticity is ascribed, one is given an implicit description of the state of the 'friend of God', the 'slave' who has 'drawn near' to God, to the point where God loves him. The saying begins with this: 'I declare war upon whosoever opposes one of My friends', a 'declaration' which alerts us to deeper implications of the 'nearness' to God enjoyed by His 'friends', the saints. Then it proceeds to speak about two degrees of nearness attained by the creatures of God, one which is defined in relation to the performance of obligatory devotion; the other, in relation to devotions voluntarily given, over and above what is obligatory. The former type of nearness is granted by means of forms of devotion that are beloved by God, whereas in the latter case, it is the soul drawn close who is the object of God's love, and this love implies union: 'My slave draws near to Me through nothing I love more than that which I have made obligatory for him. *My slave never ceases to draw near to Me through supererogatory acts until I love him. And when I love him, I am his hearing by which he hears, his sight by which he sees, his hand by which he grasps, and his foot by which he walks.*[54] (emphasis added)

At this point it might be useful to see the way in which al-Ghazzālī interprets this saying, one of the most oft-quoted in the works of the Sufis. Book six of volume four of his *Iḥyāʾ* is entitled 'The Book of Love (*maḥabba*) and longing and intimacy and contentment'. In his discussion on the love of God for man, he writes, in theological mode, that whereas one can legitimately apply the same word, love, both to man and to God, the meaning of the word changes depending on the agent of love. Human love is an inclination (*mayl*) of the soul towards that which is in harmony with it, beauty both outward and inward, seeking from another the consummation of love, for its perfection cannot be achieved within itself—and such love cannot be ascribed to God, in whom all perfections are infinitely and absolutely realized. However, at this point al-Ghazzālī shifts into a completely different mode of discourse, and asserts that God's love is absolutely real, and that His love is not for another—such is inconceivable—but rather is for Himself: for His own Essence, qualities and acts: for 'there is nothing in being except His Essence and His acts'.[55] Hence, when the Qurʾān asserts that 'He loves them' (5:54), this means that 'God does indeed love them [people], but in reality He loves nothing other than Himself, in the sense that He is the totality [of being], and there is nothing in being apart from Him.'[56] Al-Ghazzālī proceeds to show how this love of God for Himself in and as the totality of creatures most clearly manifests itself, and this he does by reference to the saying quoted above: God is the hearing, sight, hand and foot of the one He loves, and the one He loves is the one who draws close to Him

[54] *Ṣaḥīḥ al-Bukhārī, Kitāb al-riqāq,* no.2117, p.992.

[55] *Laysa fi'l-wujūd illā dhātuhu wa afʿāluhu.*

[56] *Bi-ḥaqq yuḥibbuhum, fa-innahu laysa yuḥibbu illā nafsahu, ʿalā maʿnā an-nahu al-kull, wa anna laysa fi'l-wujūd ghayrahu.* Al-Ghazzālī cites the saying of Shaykh Saʿīd al-Mayhinī here. *Iḥyāʾ ʿulūm al-dīn* (Beirut: Dār al-Jīl, 1992), book 6, part 4, vol. 5, p.221.

through supererogatory prayer.

This capacity to attain this degree of 'nearness', is itself an expression of the eternally real love of God. According to al-Ghazzālī, this perfect and eternal love of God creates the human being in a disposition which seeks proximity to Him, and furnishes him with access to the pathways leading to the removal of the veils separating him from God, such that he comes to 'see' God by means of God Himself. 'And all this', says al-Ghazzālī, 'is the act of God, and a grace bestowed upon him [God's creature]: and such is what is meant by God's love of him.'[57] This enlightening grace of God towards His creatures is constitutive of His love for them, a love which in reality is nothing other than His love for Himself; and there is a clear link between this divine love of God for Himself and the highest realization of mystical *tawḥīd*.

Although on the surface the saying appears to make God's love the result of contingent actions—the voluntary performance of religious acts of devotion—divine love is the eternally pre-existent reality, for God is not subject to change: all that can change is the perception of the soul, which, mysteriously, comes to see its own illusory nature and the unique reality proper to God; evidently, only God can 'see' this reality, whence the saying: God becomes the 'eye' by which the saint sees, and the saint 'sees' both his own nothingness and the sole reality of God. In other words, it is only possible to assert that God loves Himself as and through His creatures, from the point of view of one who has gained this 'proximity' to God and thus comes to a realization that it is indeed God and not himself who 'sees' through him, 'hears' through him, and so on. Such a knowledge is only granted, according to al-Ghazzālī in another treatise, to those who have seen through the illusory nature of their own existence, and this can only occur as a consequence of realizing the state of *fanā'*, extinction, annihilation, in God. It is this that the highest category of knowers of God undergoes; it is this *self-denouement* that provides them with the ultimate realization of the principle of *tawḥīd*:

> 'They become intoxicated with such an intoxication that the ruling authority of their rational faculty is overthrown. Hence one of them says, 'I am the Real!' (*anā'l-Ḥaqq*),

[57] *Iḥyā'*, pp.221-222.

> another, 'Glory be to me, how great is my station!'[58] ... When this state gets the upper hand, it is called 'extinction' in relation to the one who possesses it. Or rather, it is called 'extinction from extinction', since the possessor of the state is extinct from himself and from his own extinction. For he is conscious neither of himself in that state, nor of his own unconsciousness of himself. If he were conscious of his own unconsciousness, then he would [still] be conscious of himself. In relation to the one immersed in it, this state is called 'unification' (*ittiḥād*) according to the language of metaphor, or is called 'declaring God's unity' (*tawḥīd*) according to the language of reality.'[59]

Ittiḥād, or 'unification' implies the bringing together of two distinct entities—and this is 'metaphorical' (*majāzī*), a means of expressing a reality that transcends the level at which duality has any meaning; moreover, it is *shirk* to assert that man can become one with God, or that God becomes one with man. *Tawḥīd*, on the other hand is the realization of the oneness of reality, and by that very token, the disappearance of the illusion of multiplicity. The disappearance of this illusion is predicated upon the disappearance of the individual, for individuality implies existential separation, hence multiplicity. It is this which is granted by the state of *fanāʾ*, the state of 'disappearance'—to 'dis-appear' is to render non-manifest. It is only from the vantage point of this state—or rather, the vantage point of the trace left by the state on the heart and mind of the individual once he returns to self-awareness—that one can authoritatively assert that God alone is; that, despite appearances to the contrary, it is He alone who acts and is acted upon, who loves and is beloved, by Himself, in Himself.

What we see here is a far more radical vision of divine oneness than that which emerges from the theological perspective of unity. While the theological view of the all-exclusive oneness of God, with its stress on the transcendence of the One, renders it difficult to speak meaningfully of God loving His creatures, the mystical vision of the all-inclusive oneness of God—complementing and not denying

58 These are famous theopathic or ecstatic utterances (*shaṭḥ*) by Ḥallāj and Bāyazīd Bisṭāmī, respectively.

59 *Al-Ghazālī—The Niche of Lights*, Tr. David Buchman (Provo, Utah: Brigham Young University Press, 1998), pp. 17-18.

exclusivity—together with its stress on divine immanence—again, complementing and not denying transcendence—makes it impossible to avoid the assertion that God's love for His creatures is not just real, it is absolute, unconditional and eternal, being in fact nothing but His love for Himself through the apparent reality of His creatures.

The love of God for Himself through His creation assumes an altogether transformative power from the point of view of *walāya*, that sanctity which is the fruit of the purest *tawḥīd*, which in turn is predicated upon the complete effacement of all that is other than God—only then can one speak about God's love for Himself *through* His creatures. The creatures are to be empty of themselves if this love is to have free passage through them; there is no question of consummation of divine love without human extinction. Love becomes a transformative power and not just a destructive one, as might be wrongly inferred from the stress on effacement, annihilation, extinction, attained through the state of *fanāʾ*. For the individual rises from the ashes of extinction, living in a station of 'subsistence' (*baqāʾ*), which itself is rendered a transparent veil over the fully realized vision of the one-and-only reality of God. To say that the saint subsists within God is to say that God subsists within the saint, and for that very reason, the graces of divine love and divine knowledge radiate from God through the saint to the whole of creation. To see a saint is thus to witness something of the divine reality which he has rendered transparent by his very effacement in that reality. Whence the extraordinary saying of the Prophet in relation to the saint, *par excellence*, of Islam, his cousin and son-in-law, ʿAlī: 'To gaze upon the face of ʿAlī is an act of worship (*al-naẓar ilā wajhi ʿAlī ʿibāda*).[60]

The infinite love of this unique reality flows from itself to itself through ceaseless waves of creative manifestation which are lovingly reabsorbed into the ocean from which they momentarily arose: *Truly we are God's and truly unto Him we return* (2:156). Love, on all planes and all degrees, is thus inseparable from death: *amor et mors*. To die for the sake of the Beloved, however, is to effect a rebirth,

[60] This saying is transmitted both in Shīʿī and Sunnī sources. For the latter, see for example Jalāl al-Dīn al-Suyūṭī, *Taʾrīkh al-khulafāʾ*, where the saying is given on the authority of the first caliph, Abū Bakr tr. H.S. Jarrett, *History of the Caliphs* (Amsterdam: Oriental Press, 1970), p.97; al-Ḥākim al-Nīsābūrī, *Mustadrak ʿalā 'l-ṣaḥīḥayn* ((Beirut: Dār Iḥyāʾ al-Turāth al-ʿArabī, 2002), p.938, no. 4736. See our *Justice and Remembrance—Introducing the Spirituality of Imam ʿAlī* (London: I.B. Tauris, 2006), for this and several other sayings of the Prophet regarding ʿAlī.

not of oneself, but of the Beloved within oneself, the Beloved that is now liberated from the prison of the separated self, the Beloved that is now revealed behind the veil of the illusory ego. To die to the unreality of one's ego is to make way for the unitive reality of love to be born within and through oneself. In a divine utterance transmitted by ᶜAlī we are allowed to glimpse this miraculous life after death, this Love after death:

> Who seeketh Me
> findeth Me,
> Who findeth Me
> knoweth Me.
>
> Who knoweth Me
> loveth Me,
> Who loveth Me,
> I love.
>
> Whom I love, I slay
> Whom I slay, I must requite,
> Whom I must requite,
> Myself am the Requital.[61]

[61] This saying is found in many sources, Sunnī and Shīᶜī alike. See for example the Qur'ān commentary of Ismāᶜīl Ḥaqqī Bursevī, *Rūḥ al-bayān*, on Q 2:179 ('In the law of proportionate retaliation (*qiṣāṣ*), there is life for you'), where he quotes the final part of this saying (he quotes it again in his comment on 26:145); see also the commentary of Mullā Ṣadrā (Ṣadr al-Muta'allihīn), *Tafsīr Mullā Ṣadrā* on 3:170. The English translation given here is from Abū Bakr Sirāj ad-Dīn, *The Book of Certainty*, p.75.

A Common Word for a Common Future

by Miroslav Volf

Gloomy Clouds—Sun's Rays

Most people today see a heavy and dangerous storm of tensions between Christians and Muslims as menacing the world. Since the Crusades, relations between these two faith communities—currently comprised of just slightly under half the human race—have rarely been at a lower point than they are today. Tensions, deep conflicts, and often murderous violence between them are leaving a trail of blood and tears as well as a mounting deposit of deeply painful and potently dangerous memories. These clashes undermine the hopes and efforts of many to live in peace, to flourish as individuals and communities. Worse still, this stunted living enveloped in hopelessness often sucks people even deeper down the whirlpool of violence.

But many Muslims and Christians sense a new wind of hope beginning to blow—they feel the warm sun's rays penetrating the stormy gloom around us. *A Common Word Between Us and You* —likely the most important interfaith document to appear in the past four decades—is one such ray shining through the barely parting clouds. The central message of this Muslim letter, endorsed by some of the most prominent Muslim leaders worldwide and addressed to Christian leaders across the planet, is as simple as it is profound: What binds Muslims and Christians together is common belief in the Oneness of God and the commitment to love God and neighbor. This same belief and the same commitment, of course, bind Christians and Muslims to their elder sibling Judaism, the original Abrahamic faith that has transmitted to the world these two divine commandments in the first place.

Signs of Hope

As a reminder, *A Common Word* was issued not just in an atmosphere of stormy relations between Muslims and Christians but as a response to what many Muslims have experienced as a Christian provocation.

Its occasion was the famous Regensburg address of Pope Benedict XVI delivered in September 2006. In it Pope Benedict quoted the Byzantine emperor Manuel II Paleologos, who in a debate with a learned Persian Muslim said: "Show me just what Muhammad brought that was new, and there you will find things only evil and inhuman, such as his command to spread by the sword the faith he preached." Many devout Muslims worldwide felt insulted.

Yet despite the perceived provocation, uttered in a context of deteriorating relations between Muslims and Christians—perhaps in part because of the provocation—key Muslim leaders gathered around *A Common Word* did not respond in kind. Notwithstanding the present conflicts, they chose to speak of benevolence and beneficence, not to express hatred or to seek revenge. They turned their felt provocation into an occasion to send into the wider world what seemed to many an utterly novel idea: For Muslims, the commitment to love God and neighbor is central, and they share it with Christians (as well as Jews—religiously, their common elder siblings). It has been said that God knows how to write straight even on crooked lines. The signatories of *A Common Word* also wrote "straight" on the crooked line of deep tensions. The whole Christian community, indeed the whole world, should be grateful to them.

I trust it will not be taken as self-serving if I mention another, much smaller ray that penetrated the stormy clouds of Christian-Muslim relations. It was the Yale response to *A Common Word,* titled "Loving God and Neighbor Together." What's significant about the Yale response, of course, is not so much that it was written—rather, that it was endorsed by over five hundred Christian leaders, many of whom are heads of large, worldwide constituencies comprised of literally hundreds of millions of believers. Why did they endorse it? Because their holy book tells them to live in peace with all people and because they sensed a danger of global proportions if a just peace between Muslims and Christians does not triumph over tensions and injustice. The Yale response, though early and widely endorsed, was not the only response to *A Common Word.* Many Christians from all corners of the world have responded favorably as well, most recently and with great theological depth and ecumenical sensitivity Archbishop of Canterbury Rowan Williams. The broad support of *A Common Word* in the Muslim community and the favorable response to it in the Christian community suggest that we may be poised for a sea of change in Muslim-Christian relations. A day of transition from deep conflicts to mutually beneficial coexistence may be dawning.

Commonalities and Differences

Lest someone suppose that this assessment is a too-quick and somewhat cheap triumph of religion over conflict, let me make plain what I am not saying about the significance of finding commonality between Christianity and Islam in the dual command of love. First, to have the dual command of love in common does not equate with amalgamation into one and the same religion. Even if there is significant agreement on love of God and neighbor, many differences remain—differences that are not accidental to each faith but which define them. Some of these differences concern their basic understandings of God, love and neighbor. For instance, Christians believe that the One and Unique God, who is utterly exalted above all creation, is the Holy Trinity, and that God has shown unconditional love for humanity in that Jesus Christ as God's Lamb bore the sin of the world. Muslims generally do not share these beliefs. Other differences concern the sources of revelation. Muslims revere the Prophet Muhammad as the "Seal of the prophets" and the Holy Quran as sacred Scripture. Christians do not. Significant agreement on love of God and neighbor does not erase significant differences. What agreement does is this: It enables those of deep faith to respect and protect others despite these differences, leads them to get to know each other in their differences, and helps them live together harmoniously notwithstanding their differences.

Second, to agree on the dual command of love is not to say that all the practical problems causing tensions between these two communities have now been resolved. Many thorny issues remain—large and small wars in which Christians and Muslims are involved, persecution and lack of full religious freedom, problems concerning evangelism and *da'wa,* and many others. The common commitment to love of God and neighbor does not eliminate all conflicts. What common commitment does is this: It provides a basis on which Muslims and Christians can productively discuss and overcome these conflicts.

Thirdly, and equally significantly, agreement on the dual command of love encourages each community to hold the other accountable to its best insights and commitments. A Muslim as the target of Christian verbal attacks can now say to a Christian, "How can you claim that you love me when you only speak ill of my God, when you malign my Prophet, and when you despise my way of life?" A Christian convert from Islam can now say to a hostile Muslim, "How can you say that you love me if you want to kill me because I have followed my conscience and embraced the Christian faith?" The common commitment to love of neighbor has real consequences on the ground. If practiced, it has the potential to defuse many serious conflicts of a global reach (such as that of the Danish cartoons of the Prophet Muhammad).

Transforming Love and Orienting Faith

But can one bring about a shift from what feels like a clash of civilizations to conviviality of faith traditions by promoting what some people may deem as an esoteric feeling of human devotion to God and a soft and nebulous sentiment of love? Should we not be grappling with the harder realities of life? Should we not be discussing poverty and economic development, freedom of expression, education, stewardship of the environment, pluralism and democracy, the balance of power, resistance to extremists of all stripes, or modes of countering violence with effective force? If religion has anything to do with conflicts between Christians and Muslims, the critics may continue, religious passions stemming from single-minded devotion to God as the champion of one's cause are the source of these conflicts, not a means to overcome them. Less religion is what we need, not more. Take God out of it all, critics conclude, and let people keep religious devotion locked in the privacy of their hearts, and restrict the virtues and delights of love to friendship and family. Let instead individual and national interests, as well as the balance of power tempered by the claims of hard-nosed justice, regulate worldly affairs.

So what worldly good can come of promoting love of God and love of neighbor? Why do we see a sign of hope in *A Common Word?* Partly because, properly understood, love is not a soft and a nebulous emotion but a tough, practical virtue of benevolence and beneficence toward all, a virtue of which justice is an absolutely integral part. And religious faith is not impractical at all! For people of faith, Christians and Muslims alike, God is a motivating and sustaining power, the Holy One who gives meaning, weight, and direction to their life. In the current jargon, faith is what "makes them tick."

Faith Matters

It's not just love's toughness and the orienting character of faith, however, that makes these two loves—love of God and love of neighbor—socially important. Consider the undiminished vibrancy of faith in the contemporary world. To the surprise of many—notably those who believe that religion will gradually retreat before the light of reason and the wonders of technological development—the world today is becoming a more religious rather than a less religious place. The world is not progressively secularizing; to the contrary, it is desecularizing. The trend is likely to continue into the foreseeable future.

Religious faiths, notably Christianity and Islam, are reasserting themselves in two important senses. First, the number of their adherents in the world is growing in absolute and relative terms as compared to non-religious worldviews. Second, religious people increasingly consider their faith not as simply a private affair but a significant shaper of their public engagements. Religion matters profoundly, and matters in the public as well as the private sphere. I hope this claim will not be heard as a statement of religious triumphalism. I am aware that religion is often employed to wrap appallingly base causes in the aura of the sacred and to legitimize, even promote, violence. My point is not to deny this obvious fact. Neither is it to suggest that disbelief will be pushed out of existence or that non-believers' freedoms ought to be restricted. My aim is rather to remind that religion matters and to point to a significant and unavoidable consequence of this fact.

What is this consequence? Negatively, if religion matters, no peace between religious people will be achieved by pretending that it is merely a veil hiding some undeniable economic, political, or other interest. Positively, if religion matters, we have to find resources for the conviviality of religious people within in each faith tradition itself.

Deep Faith and Social Pluralism

It is because faith matters that the *Common Word* initiative is so significant. First, *A Common Word* points both Muslims and Christians to what is undeniably essential in each faith and common to both—love of God and love of neighbor. Second, it shows how that which is essential in each faith and common to both has the power to bind them together because it encourages—indeed, demands—that their adherents seek the good of others, not just their own good. If it is true that the dual command of love binds the faiths together, the consequences are revolutionary in the best sense of the word. We no longer have to say, "The deeper your faith is, the more at odds with others you will be!" (provided, of course, that "deep faith" means not just "emotionally strong faith" but "intelligent and informed faith"). To the contrary, we must say: "The deeper your faith is, the more in harmony with others you will live!" A deep faith no longer leads to clashes—it fosters conviviality.

What some people deride as an impractical and soft commitment to love God and neighbor—but what is really attachment to the Source of all reality and practice of beneficence—has real-life effects in defusing conflicts and fostering conviviality. It makes possible what would otherwise remain unattainable in a world of personally vibrant and socially assertive faiths. We can embrace deep faith while at the same time respecting the rights and promoting the well-being of those who do not share it. Deep faith expresses itself in love, and love, understood as benevolence and beneficence, leads to respect of and struggle for others' rights. Put differently, and maybe surprisingly to some, commitment to the properly understood love of God and neighbor makes deeply religious persons, because they are deeply religious, into dedicated social pluralists. When Christians and Muslims commit themselves to practicing the dual command of love, they are not satisfying some private religious fancy; instead, they are actively fostering conviviality in our ineradicably pluralistic world that is plagued by deep divisions. They are making possible the constructive collaboration of people of different faiths in the common public space for the common good.

Planetary Common Good

The significance of the *Common Word* initiative goes beyond relations between Muslims and Christians. The initiative holds the potential for providing a good platform for Christians and Muslims together to engage great and troubling problems facing humanity today. If God's mercy encompasses all, or, as Christians might say, if God's love is universal, then so should the love of Muslims and Christians be—love for all humanity that is concerned for all aspects of every person's life. We live in a thoroughly interconnected and interdependent world that is and knows itself as one world (as we have been made painfully aware by the ongoing deep financial crisis, and as the ecological crisis attests). We're all in the same rocking boat, so to speak, and the good of one is the good of all; the ill of one is the ill of all. It is also a world caught in a whirlwind of unprecedented change. It seems that nothing is stable and that everything can—and eventually will—be overturned.

In the context of such highly dynamic and thoroughgoing interdependence, a "common word" between Muslims and Christians should not just be about mutual relations between these two faiths. It should be also, and maybe above all, about the common good for the little boat that is our common world. In addition to sitting face-to-face and trying to make peace with one another, we need to start walking shoulder to shoulder in trying to heal the deep wounds and inspire the noble hopes of all people in our common world. Human flourishing and even human survival may depend on it.

An Encounter of Seven

But what would it take for Muslims and Christians to have a common word with one another aimed at a better common future? How can we make fruitful the encounters of those committed to God and each other as neighbors?

Someone has said, somewhat surprisingly, that in an encounter between you and me, *four* are always involved, not just two. Two of those four are, obviously, you and I. But also present are my image of you and your image of me. If this is so, then an encounter is fruitful when my image of you has become more as you truly are, and your image of me has become more as I truly am. That's a helpful way to think about encounters between people of different faiths. It isn't quite complete, however.

In every encounter *seven* are involved—a perfect number for Christians. There are you and I, and there's my image of you and your image of me—the obvious two and somewhat surprising four.

But there's also my image of myself (which may not be true to who I am and may be very much *un*like who *you* think I am). And there's your image of yourself (which may not be true to who you are and may be very much *un*like who *I* think you are). So that's six in one encounter. The consequence? I have to learn to *see myself as I truly am*, not just demand that *you* see me as I am (which is often a demand that you see me not as I *truly* am but as I *think* I am). Similarly, you have to learn to *see yourself as you truly are,* not just demand that *I* see you as you are (which is, again, often a demand that I see you not as you *truly* are but as you *think* you are).

But I spoke of *seven* in every encounter? Where does the seventh come from? In every encounter there is also another One present, the categorically unique and utterly incomparable One, the absolutely truthful and infinitely merciful One. God is present in every encounter. As the truthful One, God sees each of us truthfully rather than distorting our identities. And God's truthful perception of us demands our truthful self-perception as well as the truthful perceiving of others. Further, as the merciful One, God desires us to be merciful in all our dealings with one another and with the world. Indeed, God desires of us to be *as* truthful and *as* merciful with ourselves, with one another, and with the world as He himself is truthful and merciful.

If God is always involved in any fruitful encounter, then it is clear that the seventh one is really the First One—not first in a series, but the first one who makes the series possible at all. Fruitful encounter between those who love God and neighbor is possible only because the God of love makes it possible—makes possible the encounter as well as the love of God and of neighbor around which it takes place. Hence both our love of God and our love of neighbor appropriately must start with the recognition that we and our world are loved by the God of infinite love. The dual command of love is rooted in the simple and the most sublime reality of the God who "is love," as the Epistle of John states.

A Mighty Tree?

It is not too much to say that the *Common Word* initiative, with its emphasis on the dual command of love, has the potential of becoming a historic watershed defining the relations between the two numerically largest faiths in the world today for the good of all humanity. But will it? Will *A Common Word* be a seed that has fallen on unfertile ground and dies? Or will it grow into a great tree under whose branches many will be able to find shade? Will it remain just a document that gathers the dust of history? Or will it become a common platform from which to address effectively many areas of tension between Muslims and Christians, as well as many of the burning issues in our interconnected world?

Which of these possibilities will be realized? If Muslims and Christians embrace the initiative and commit themselves to love of God and neighbor, the *Common Word* initiative will open up a new future for Muslims, Christians and Jews—a future in which many swords will be turned into plowshares and clashes replaced by conviviality.

Seeking Common Ground between Muslims and Christians

by Ibrahim Kalin

Given the difficulties of interreligious and intercultural dialogue between Islam and the West, a historic step was taken in Rome on November 4-6, 2008. The first Seminar of the Catholic-Muslim Forum was held at the Vatican with the participation of about 60 Muslim and Catholic religious leaders and scholars from around the world. For two days in workshops closed to the public, the participants discussed the love of God, love of the neighbor, human dignity and mutual respect in the two traditions of Islam and Christianity. On November 6th, the delegation was received by Pope Benedict XVI inside the Vatican where Mustafa Ceric, the Grand Mufti of Bosnia and Herzegovina, and Seyyed Hossein Nasr, the renowned scholar of Islam, spoke on behalf of the Muslim delegation representing the signatories of the *Common Word.*

Establishing religious and cultural accord is difficult anywhere in the world. This is especially true for the long and checkered relationship between Islam and Christianity. Islam's meteoric rise to the stage of world history in the 7th century when Christianity was struggling both in the East and in Europe created a sense of rivalry and urgency among Western Christians. Islam's claim of restoring Abrahamic monotheism and rejection of the Christian Trinity was received as a theological challenge. Its rapid expansion into areas that were once under the Byzantine rule led to a heightened sense of political and military threat. Finally, the dominance of Islamic culture and civilization after the 10th and 11th centuries was a cause of alarm to many Christians in Europe. Periods of peaceful co-existence in places like Andalusia, Baghdad and Istanbul have not changed this fact. As works of Southern, Daniel, Kedar, Tolan and others show, the attitudes of pre-modern Christendom towards Islam remained mostly hostile and exclusivist, and some of these attitudes continue to form the views and perceptions current in Western societies today.

Going beyond the Regensburg Debacle

The Pope Benedict's 2006 Regensburg address came as a shock to many in the Muslim world because it reiterated the old misconceptions of Islam as an irrational and violent religion. The Regensburg speech claimed that Islamic faith left little or no room for human ("natural") reason and asked its followers to blindly follow a stern and rule-driven God. This implied that Islam was unable to develop a rational discourse about its religious tenets and thus invited its followers to "submit" to God rather than to think about or love Him. Furthermore, it claimed that Islam spread through violence, which is an extension of its irrational nature. On both counts, Christians, the Pope implied, cannot have religious or theological dialogue with Muslims. Even though the Pope Benedict was quoting some provocative medieval sources about Islam, it was clear that his typology of religions accorded a place to Islam only as a culture, not a religion. In addition to *Salt of the Earth: The Church at the End of the Millennium* (1997), Benedict reiterated the same point in an address to a Muslim audience in August 2005 where he used a distinctively socio-cultural language to describe the importance of Muslim-Christian relations.

There are two main problems with these arguments. Firstly, the claims of irrationality and violence are based on a shallow and distorted reading of Islamic intellectual and political history. Neither the strict literalism of the now defunct school of Ibn Hazm mentioned in the Regensburg speech nor the military conquests of medieval Muslim empires are sufficient for such a judgment. What is intriguing is that the long and honorable tradition of first rate Catholic scholarship on Islam is alarmingly absent in some of the Vatican statements about Islam and Muslims. Secondly, one can easily use the two arguments of the Regensburg speech against the Catholic Church itself. As a matter of fact, it was primarily arguments of this sort which Enlightenment thinkers used to envisage a post-Christian Europe in the 17th and 18th centuries.

The *Common Word* letter, out of which the first Seminar of the Catholic-Muslim Forum developed, addressed these and other issues to open up new lines of communication between Muslims and Christians. Taking its cue from the Qur'an, it claimed that there is a ground for theological engagement while religious differences are to be admitted as part of a genuine dialogue and ethics of co-existence. At another level, this is a call for the acknowledgement of a Judeo-

Christian-Islamic tradition. As the Pope underlined in his address to the Muslim delegation, "we can and must be worshippers of the one God who created us and is concerned about each person in every corner of the world". In addition to the intricacies of Christian and Muslim theology, there are also grounds for practical cooperation between the two largest religious and cultural communities of the world.

In any interfaith engagement, one wonders if one should concentrate on practical issues and avoid theological debate as it will likely not go anywhere. Many engaged in interfaith dialogue prefer to deal with practical issues with the hope that this would produce concrete results on the ground. Interreligious dialogue, however, cannot function in a "beyond-the-truth" kind of attitude because, for one, all religions lay a claim to the truth (regardless of how one understands it). One has to take these claims seriously. Secondly, one is expected to remain loyal to one's tradition in broad outlines while reaching out to the other(s); otherwise a dialogue without a center would be without meaning and substance. Plus, it will have no representation and thus no impact on the larger community. On both counts, the Vatican meeting exceeded expectations. The meetings, speeches and the Final Declaration are punctuated with points of theological reasoning and practical concerns. This is an encouraging outcome and shows that careful and patient work can break new ground in bridging the gap between Muslim and Christian communities.

Differences, Obstacles, Family Resemblances

One of the outcomes of the Vatican meeting is the recognition that one does not need uniformity to seek common grounds. The theological and historical differences between Islam and Christianity are considerable but not impossible to discuss. The Christian view of Christ as the Son of God and suffering savior is different from Islamic notions of salvation and eschatology. In his *Truth and Tolerance*: *Christian Belief and World Religions* (2004), Benedict affirms that "faith in Jesus Christ as the only Savior and the indivisibility of Christ and the Church is the foundation". The Muslim concept of Jesus, however, remains within the confines of Islamic prophetology and accords him a central place in the history of revelation. As for the Virgin Mary, she is mentioned more in the Qur'an than in the Bible and her name decorates the *mihrab*s of countless mosques around the world. Together with Fatimah and other women of early Islamic history, Mary is also one of the towering figures of Islamic spirituality. The Christian tradition on the other hand rejects the Qur'an as a revelation and the Prophet Muhammad as a messenger of God. While even the most bigoted religious zealots in the Muslim world would not say anything against Jesus or Mary, the Prophet Muhammad is routinely insulted by numerous Christian circles. Fortunately, the Catholic-Muslim Forum took a clear position against "any form of mockery or ridicule" of the sacred figures and symbols of Islam and Christianity.

Both traditions emphasize love as an essential quality of the Divine but assign different functions to its application in human life. Unconditional love is central to Christian theology because "God is love" (John 4, 16). Expanding upon the same principle of love, Islamic scriptures also stress mercy (*raḥmah*) and justice (*'adl*) as complimentary qualities of the Divine. A *ḥadīth* of the Prophet Muhammad, quoted in the Final Declaration, states that "God's loving compassion for humanity is even greater than that of a mother for her child" (Muslim, Bab al-Tawba: 21). Islam and Christianity agree that the Divinely sanctioned love guides all commandments and extends to all of God's creation. While everybody accepts the command to "love thy neighbor" as extending to all human beings including those outside one's spiritual communion, the challenge is how one puts it into practice with patience and consistency. Despite the assurances of Catholic and Muslim theologians, one wonders why and how these two religions that place love and mercy at the heart of their theologies can harbor so much mistrust, fear and occasionally hatred of one another.

Besides theology, the two religions have followed different trajectories in their encounter with modernity and secularization. From Jacques Maritain to Pope Benedict XVI, Catholic theologians appear to have embraced the basic values of secular modernity on "personalism", human rights and social ethics in order to secure a breathing space for the Christian faith in an increasingly secularizing, individualistic and materialistic world. Yet seeking to use the arguments of a post-Christian philosophy in favor of traditional Christianity has not always worked to save the Church from the onslaught of an aggressively secular and skeptical age. A major philosophical difference separates the post-Vatican II notion of the "human person" from that of Islam. The Vatican's concept of the dignity and inalienable rights of the person echoes well with the broad outlines of Kant's post-

Christian and post-metaphysical theology. And it can be perfectly justified on the basis of Biblical and Qur'anic pronouncements about the unique position of the human state in the great circle of creation. But it comes close to erecting a subjectivist theology on the basis of a secular anthropocentric humanism. In either case, the modern autonomous individual and his/her "choices" in the Weberian sense of the term seem to have the final say over what counts as the basis of normative theology.

Modern Islamic thought has largely stayed away from embracing the secular humanism of the Enlightenment. Even in the case of such modernist figures as Muhammad Iqbal and Fazlur Rahman we do not find either an anthropocentric cosmology or a notion of religion reduced to social utility. 'Muslim personalism', attempted by Iqbal, Lahbabi and others, remains within the confines of Islam's monotheism and moral communalism. Despite Pope Benedict's criticisms of extreme secularization and rampant relativism shared by many Muslims, the way in which Islam and Catholicism are dealing with the challenges of our secular age reflects different philosophical positions.

Religious Freedom and the Legacy of Colonialism

Similarities and differences extend to practical issues as well. While Christians insist on freedom of religion and conscience as a universal human right, which the majority of Muslims accepts, missionaries interpret it as a license to proselytize in Muslim countries, which Muslims reject. This is where Pope Bendict's view of mission and dialogue as the two sides of the same coin enters in. While it is true that every religion is missionary in the sense of witnessing one's faith, there are worlds of differences in the way religious communities make their message (and witnessing) available to others. Many in the Muslim world see the aggressive missionary work of European and American religious organizations as part and parcel of the Western power structure and indeed instrumental to it, and denounce it as a continuation of 19th century colonialism. Given the painful memories of European colonialism and the political realities of the current world order, which is dominated by countries that are at least nominally Christian, it is not possible to speak of religious freedom in the abstract.

The deplorable human rights record of Muslim countries makes life miserable for both Muslim and non-Muslim communities. The reality of corrupt and autocratic regimes in Muslim countries does not prove the absence of a democratic and participatory culture in Muslim societies. Rather it points to a source of extreme frustration among the Muslim masses. Nevertheless, none of these should be an excuse for the oppression and humiliation of non-Muslim communities in Muslim majority countries. Muslim nations have a religious, moral and civic duty to work for the protection of the rights of their non-Muslim neighbors and fellow citizens as equal members of society. But it is obvious that equal rights and civil liberties will not be secured for everyone until an effective system of representative democracy is established for Muslim countries. This, in turn, brings us back to the global balance of power that dictates the parameters of regional and national politics in much of the Muslim world.

At this point, the Muslim world needs to recover the spirit of cosmopolitan Islam which generated and nurtured the classical Islamic civilization. Striking a balance between recognizing the plurality of religious and cultural communities on the one hand, and remaining loyal to one's own spiritual tradition on the other was the hallmark of Muslim societies from the greater Mesopotamia to al-Andalus. Such cosmopolitan centers of Muslim culture as Baghdad, Damascus, Cordoba, Alexandria, Sarajevo and Istanbul were among the finest examples of the Qur'anic injunction of "striving for the common good" (*al-khayrat*) of God's creation. Responding to God's will to create diverse "nations and tribes" did not diminish but increased and deepened the Muslim sense of serving God by loving Him and one's neighbor. It is this spirit of cosmopolitan Islam that has been lost in the modern maelstrom of oppositional identities, religious formalism and profane politics.

Differences do not obviate serious intellectual engagement. The current global problems call for a dialogical conversation between Christians and Muslims as well as others. As religions have to learn to live in an increasingly pluralistic world, they are bound to listen to one another more attentively. Muslims and Christians should mobilize their resources to address the spiritual crisis and social problems of our day and age. It is encouraging to see that the Catholic-Muslim Forum has agreed to "explore the possibility of establishing a permanent Catholic-Muslim committee to coordinate responses to conflicts and other emergency situations". Such measures could prove to be vital to diffuse communal tension and misunderstanding.

Centuries of conflict, suspicion, mistrust, rivalry and violence will not be resolved over the course of several or more meetings. But the *Common Word* initiative and Pope Benedict's positive response to it represent a major step towards a "historical reconciliation" between Islam and the West. The Pope has already made some goodwill gestures before meeting with the Muslim delegation of the *Common Word* on November 6. His stance against the Iraq war, his call for a just solution to the Palestinian problem, and his positive messages during his visit to Turkey in 2007 should be seen as important steps in the right direction. But much more work remains to be done in order to bring to life the message of love of God and love of the neighbor.

Human Dignity and Mutual Respect

by Abdal Hakim Murad

Your Eminences, Excellencies, Distinguished Guests and Friends. Peace be with you, and the Mercy and Compassion of God.

Our meeting in this historic place is, God willing, a celebration and a sign of hope. Celebration as we together feast on God's revealed words, nourished and sustained to carry the message of truth and reconciliation to the communities which we represent. And hope, in the assurance that the scrutiny which Heaven assuredly directs to our deliberations and to the states of our hearts in these days will overlook our many shortcomings, and be the sign under which the best and most fruitful exchanges of our two faiths in the past will continue to inspire us, while we find new and successful means of overcoming both those misunderstandings and those errors of intention which have, in past ages, led us into conflicts displeasing to God.

It is evident to us all how close is the relationship between the great subject of our discussions yesterday and the subject which we address today. Indeed, it is this relationship which lies at the heart of the distinctiveness of the religious response to the crisis of modernity. Ours is an age in which noble efforts are made to esteem humanity, through codes of human rights and international conventions of many kinds. Yet the philosophy which, in today's prevailing secular climate, seeks to offer foundations to these efforts today seems to exist in a state of crisis. The Enlightenment, source of much that is precious to our contemporary understanding of human dignity, was attacked in its day by religious and also some secular thinkers who doubted the claims of a purely secular ethic, and of a categoric imperative rooted in an immense optimism about the moral capacity of unaided reason and science. That pessimism has, in part, proved reasonable. Europe, cradle

Address delivered to the Catholic-Muslim Forum November 5, 2008

of the Enlightenment, is today the cradle of a postmodern relativism of a most virulent kind. The spirits released from the Pandora's box of the *Lumières* and the *Aufklärung*, and in my own country by Locke and Hume, have proven, in some cases, to be allies to the angels; but in others to be unmistakeably from the infernal realms of subversion and enmity. Europe—and I speak here as a European—is in crisis, and believers, who for so long, sometimes rightly, and sometimes cravenly, stood against the Enlightenment project, are called upon today to heal its deep pain. Christians and Muslims, as followers of Europe's two largest religions, must surely work together as never before in finding a remedy. We must also work to ensure that Europe's heart-sickness, expressed today in an almost unrivalled religious indifference, is not exported to the world.

This is, in fact, where I wish to direct my remarks. As a citizen and advocate of the European Union, I find myself part of a tragically godless society. Recently a sociologist published a book with the title *The Death of Christian Britain*, and this hurts me deeply, because in fact what is dying is the set of monotheistic convictions and a life of prayer and human giving that as Muslims we wish to see thrive around us. Yet I am also a member of Islam. That combination of the European and the Islamic is one that would be less difficult were Europe to be more faithful to the Christian dimension of its heritage. I prefer to live in a Christian society than in a secular one.

This sense of loss motivates my own particular commitment to the *Common Word* process. As you are aware, the meeting of this Forum here in Rome is one consequence of the initiative launched a year ago by Muslim scholars who, distressed by the current state of the world, offered a hand of support and goodwill to the spiritual heads of Christendom. My own reason for signing, in addition to the consensus of the document's signatories that the world is in need of healing, and that Muslims are summoned to call mankind to the undying principles of love of God and of neighbour, was that I am particularly distraught by Europe's lack of faith, and the diminution of human dignity and conviviality that surely results.

If, in many inner city areas, and increasingly elsewhere, Muslims live as a significant European constituency, then there is much scope for working together against our continent's current degraded view of human vocation and destiny. And it is my belief that the Holy See's current insistence on the revival of the heritage of religious reason is entirely correct. It is important to recollect that the Catholic Church, as the world's oldest institution, has a long memory which encompasses other, earlier episodes when the prospects seemed dark. St. Benedict of Nursia, fifteen hundred years ago, lived during barbarian invasions, which seemed to threaten Europe with a polytheistic relativism, and an inhuman ethic of greed and domination. The remedy, as Benedict saw, and as he lived in the actuality of his life, was the immense power of revealed certainty defended and reinforced by reason.

With its present leadership, the Holy See is well-placed to justify its claims to be a support for true reason. And this places it, as Muslims see matters, in an ideal position for cooperation with Muslims, and surely with others, in the great task of defeating pessimism and the rule of arbitrary opinion.

Islamic theology, we now know, took some of its early methods and categories from Christians such as John Philoponus, whom we knew as Yahya al-Nahwi. Likewise, at key junctures in its own history, Christian Europe has been strengthened by the study of Islamic thinkers. Who can deny the impact of Ibn Rushd, the Sharī'ah judge of Cordoba, on Europe in the age of St. Thomas Aquinas? Or the importance of Ghazali, known to the Latins as Algazel, in his rigorous refutation of the misplaced and sometimes sub-Pagan metaphysics of Avicenna? Or the *mutakallimun*, the Muslim theologians known as 'Loquentes' in the West, whose rigour in the use of reason made them ideal interlocutors, albeit at the distance required by the culture of the time, for the most rigorous of Christian thinkers? As Europe today confronts the new barbarians, who are the postmoderns and other relativists who, not from abroad, are from an evolution of its own inner life, such a convergence can prove a vital asset. Our mutual respect can be based on the practice of shared rational confrontation of Europe's disease.

The need to base our dialogue on ideas is further underlined by the imperative of mission, so salient in both traditions. A mere collaboration on practicalities would risk muffling the theological conversation which is surely close to the heart of any true comparison of the religions' claims.

Of the great European students of Islam in the past century, many of the greatest were faithful Catholics who, following Maritain and the neo-Thomist interest in Arabic philosophy, made profound contributions to our understanding of Muslim theology. Among them we must cite the great Dominican scholars, Georges Anawati and Louis Gardet, whose 1948 manual of Islamic theology shows the importance of reason to Islamic culture, and the value of detailed comparisons with Thomism. Their Islamic focus was on Hanbalism and Ash'arism. But Maturidism, the third great school of Sunni theology, became the special concern of Josef Van Ess of Tübingen University. Van Ess has reminded us of the Maturidi insistence, present also in Ghazali and his school, on the rationality of God. In his great four-volume history of early Muslim theology, Van Ess stresses Islam's insistence on the divine ground of reason again and again. He even writes this:

> Christianity speaks of the "mysteries" of faith; Islam has nothing like that. For Saint Paul, reason belongs to the realm of the "flesh", for Muslims, reason, *'aql*, has always been the chief faculty granted human beings by God.[1]

Van Ess, and earlier Catholic scholars, have done the world an incalculable service. Secular activists of an earlier generation liked to see Islam as the worshipper of a God of unreason, a legalistic tyrant far removed from human analogy or concern. Often Islam was paired with Judaism, which an older Orientalism chose to see as analogously "Semitic" in its rejection of Hellenic or any other type of reason. Here, for instance, is Ernest Rénan, the arch-rationalist, writing in 1862:

> At the present time, the essential precondition for the spread of European civilization is the destruction of the Semitic thing *par excellence* ... the destruction of Islam ... Islam is the most complete negation of Europe: Islam is fanaticism ... The future, sirs, is therefore Europe's, and Europe's alone ... Here is eternal war, the war which will end only when the last son of Ishmael dies in misery, or is banished through terror to the depths of the desert.[2]

1 Josef Van Ess, *The Flowering of Muslim Theology* (Cambridge MA: Harvard University Press, 2006), 153-4.

2 Ernest Rénan, *De la part des peuples sémitiques dans l'histoire de la civilisation*, discours d'ouverture du cours de langue hébraique, chaldaïque et syriaque au College de France (Paris: Michel Lévy, 1862), 27-8.

Rénan, hero of the *lumières*, is convinced that Islam and Judaism can have nothing to say to the idea of human dignity. We would add that his understanding of classical Christianity is, of course, hardly more sympathetic.

By the grace of God, we have since moved on, and Muslims need to thank Catholic scholars for having banished older and effectively anti-Semitic categories in favour of an understanding of Islam as a faith in which reasoned belief in a reasonable God is central to serious theology.

Such Catholic scholars have allowed us an image of Islam which converges in key respects with modern Catholic understandings of the inherent dignity of human beings. Shaykh al-Buti has frequently referred to many of the Quranic indicants of this principle. "We have ennobled the descendents of Adam," says the Quran (17:70). Adam alone is the creature to which God orders the angels themselves to bow down (7:11). This is because God has created within him a spirit which is from God Himself (15:29; 32:9; 38:72). It is thus that our theorists, and particularly the Maturidis and Hanafis, insist that rights are innate in human beings, rather than conferred subsequently in a way that would make them entirely subject to religious confession. I would like to quote, in this connection, the words of Imam Sarakhsi, the Hanafi jurist who died in 1090:

> Upon creating human beings, God graciously bestowed upon them intelligence and the capability to carry responsibilities and rights. This was to make them ready for duties and rights determined by God. Then He granted them the right to inviolability, freedom, and property to let them continue their lives so that they can perform the duties they have shouldered. Then these rights to carry responsibility and enjoy rights, freedom, and property exist with a human being when he is born. The insane/child and the sane/adult are the same concerning these rights. This is how the proper personhood is given to him when he is born for God to charge him with the rights and duties when he is born. In this regard, the insane/child and sane/adult are equal.[3]

[3] Cited in Recep Sentürk, 'Minority Rights in Islam: From Dhimmi to Citizen,' in Shireeen T. Hunter and Huma Malik (eds.), *Islam and Human Rights: Advancing a US-Muslim Dialogue* (Washington DC: Center for International and Strategic Studies, 2005, 67-99), p.74.

This high regard for the dignity of the human person, in medieval times produced societies where non-Muslim communities flourished for centuries. Naturally the assurance was that certain rights inhered more fully in those who accepted the final revelation of God in the Quran. That assurance was in no way strange for its time, and indeed may be regarded as normative in a certain way of traditional religion. Remember, much more recently, Pope Leo XIII, author of the encyclical *Libertas*, a theologically brilliant meditation on the nature of human dignity. This is his teaching:

> Justice therefore forbids, and reason itself forbids, the State to be godless; or to adopt a line of action which would end in godlessness—namely, to treat the various religions (as they call them) alike, and to bestow upon them promiscuously equal rights and privileges.[4]

Muslims, historically, would agree with this teaching. Some continue to do so today. But just as Papal teaching, even on matters of such grave moment, must and does change, so too Muslims must today, as a matter of some urgency, address their own failures in charity towards members of minority religions. But—and here we enter less familiar ground—Muslims are also called, by the same great teaching of the inalienable dignity of man, to press their various governments to respect the rights of Muslims as well. In too many Muslim countries the right of Muslims fully to practice the faith, to wear the garments decreed by tradition in public and educational places, to construct mosques and colleges, and to call freely for the reform of rulers they consider corrupt, is curtailed. Muslims must also, as well as calling for such necessary restorations of the Quranic ideal of the dignity and honour of the Adamic creature in countries where they form a majority, stand in solidarity with Muslims who live in parts of Europe where the rise of a new pagan tribalism is making life for the Muslim faithful intolerable. We know, and receive with respect and gratitude, the commitment of Catholic clergy and faithful, to overcome the many disadvantages faced by Muslim believers in Europe, most particularly in municipalities which are controlled by far-right political formations.

I have returned, as is evident, to my theme of the tragedy of Europe. I have already indicated my belief that, as supporters of the

4 Pope Leo XIII, *Libertas*, 21.

People of the Book, we lament Europe's spiritual crisis, and wish the Churches well in their struggle to heal it. I call to mind the writing of the Catholic conscience of Belgium, Jacques Neirynck. In his novel *The Siege of Brussels (Le siège de Bruxelles)*, Neirynck depicts a nightmarish future in which chauvinism has brought about the persecution and expulsion of Belgium's hated Muslim minority; but he closes by showing how the humane mainstream voices in Islam and Christianity will ultimately prevail. My own confidence is that cooperation and mutual respect will, indeed, triumph against barbarism.

I turn now to an internal Muslim argument. Some Muslims appear to believe that this convivial, moral interaction and mutual support on issues of social concern must be detached from an attention to theology. In some cases one even hears the thought that Christianity, rooted in a belief in human sinfulness, is mistrustful of the intellect, and that its doctrines are based in a mere leap of faith. This is then contrasted with Islam which, such thinkers aver, is pre-eminently the religion of reason and of a reasonable God. One finds such perceptions in the polemics of Rashid Rida and his still very considerable school. One hears it also among less cultivated Muslims. But it is clear from any study of Catholic doctrine that natural reason is central to the Catholic intellectual enterprise. This surely means that the claim that our cooperation should be merely pragmatic, not principial, is gravely misguided. It is time that Muslims welcome cooperation with Catholics in an awareness that Catholicism, like Islam, speaks the universal language of reason.

Once this is achieved, there is much more to be achieved. Together, Muslims and Catholic Christians account for over two and a half billion souls: considerably over a third of the planet's population. The *Common Word* document stresses, from its scriptural perspective, the need not only to affirm the shared abstract principles of love of God and of neighbour, but to show the sincerity of our commitment in pastoral action. The two principles are in fact symbiotic.

We know that ours is a time of challenges to our relationship. There are Muslims, and there are Christians, who wish that our gathering here had not taken place. The *Common Word* has been condemned by some Muslim voices; and some Christians have expressed their alienation from the warm and positive Christian responses which have come from Yale, Lambeth Palace, and other centres of the Christian conscience. In some places our relationship is improving; in others it seems to be suffering from an intractable deficiency. The commandment to love God and love neighbour, which is in practice a single commandment, is not always obeyed in practice and in our hearts. There is a valid Christian fear of Muslim extremism. And there is undeniably a Muslim fear of what Hans Küng, in his book on Islam, calls America's "aggressive imperialistic foreign policy,"[5] driven, as some see it, by Christian nationalists among whom, as he says, "the crusade mentality is currently being revived."[6] We both need to acknowledge the Other's fear of us.

As Muslims, called to be open-hearted towards the founders of all three Abrahamic faiths, we are particularly pained by such tensions. The *Common Word* initiative is one expression of that pain. But we must move forward. And one admirable advocate of this has been His Eminence Cardinal Tauran, in his message for the end of Ramadan, issued six weeks ago. He entitles his letter: "Christians and Muslims: together for the dignity of the family." Here the cardinal commends past solidarity among Muslims and Catholics in the great task of defending this elemental institution of society, and prays for further collaboration in the future.

I believe that His Eminence is entirely correct, and that he has identified one of the most important areas in which our shared commitment to human dignity can find practical expression. Muslims and Catholics alike, to the scorn of secular commentators, courageously uphold an image of marriage as the proper context for the expression of human sexuality. His Holiness Pope Benedict, in his encyclical *Deus Caritas Est*, has in a timely fashion reminded the world of the dignity and holiness of human sexual desire. The erotic should be part of our spirituality, not a delation from it. The due context for this vital aspect of our dignity as incarnated beings is manifestly matrimony. And here, Muslims and Catholics will wish to differ from a certain reductionist tendency in contemporary culture to assume that men and women are different in ways that are only socially conditioned, rather than alternate, but equally valuable, expressions of aspects of the power of the One who has created humanity in the image of the Divine.

5 Hans Küng, *Islam* (Oxford, 2007), p.453.

6 Küng, p.311.

Let us borrow, in an analogising way, an insight from the Trinitarian theology of Hans Urs von Balthasar. Here the Swiss genius-theologian draws our attention to the relationship between the persons of the Trinity. He writes: "The hypostatic modes of being constitute for each other the greatest opposition we could think of [...] precisely so that the most intimate interpenetration we could think of becomes possible."[7] And, defying the impoverished modern view of gender, he goes on to identify the giving and taking of the persons of the Trinity in frankly gendered terms: the masculine principle identified with the fecundating, dynamic role, and the feminine with the receptive and the florescent.[8] Such a validation of classical Christian understandings of the mutuality of the genders in family life is clearly close, in its outcomes, to Muslim assurances; although the Trinitarian language about the inner life of God is undeniably far from Islamic faith. Shared conclusions about the value of "alternative sexualities" will surely follow.

Another area where we have already worked together to good effect is indicated in Archbishop Rowan William's splendid and detailed response to the *Common Word.* He points to the importance of the Israeli-Palestinian conflict, as "at or near the top of the list of issues that concern both Christians and Muslims all over the world." Muslims are convinced that the Apostolic See, concerned for the Catholic and other communities of Jerusalem, will stand in solidarity with Christian and Muslim believers who, while renouncing cruel and arbitrary terroristic responses, stand courageously for their right to dignity in their own land. Muslims have been immensely heartened by the courage of many Christians, such as former American President Jimmy Carter, and Archbishop Desmond Tutu of Cape Town, in condemning what they describe as Israel's apartheid policies against the Muslim and Christian communities of the occupied territories. It has been rightly said that upholding the dignity of the Palestinian people is the surest path to Muslim hearts, and we are confident that the Vatican will remember this as it attempts to advocate a peaceful and just solution for Jews, Muslims and Christians alike in the Holy Land.

[7] Hans Urs von Balthasar, *Theo-drama* II, 258, cited in Rowan Williams, "Balthasar and the Trinity," 37-50 of Edward T. Oakes SJ and David Moss (eds), *The Cambridge Companion to Hans Urs von Balthasar* (Cambridge, 2004), see p. 41.

[8] *Theo-drama* V, cited in Rowan Williams, "Balthasar and the Trinity," 45.

But there are other places in God's earth where human dignity is being outraged. It is not right for Muslims, including Arab Muslims, to call attention to the plight of the Palestinians, and to pay less attention to the victims of the current atrocities in Darfur. That scandal needs to be urgently explained and addressed. And even more recently, the tragedy in Eastern Zaire is summoning us all to joint action. One recalls, with reassurance, the good relations which were so frequently maintained between Catholics and Muslims in neighbouring Rwanda, even at the height of the appalling events of the early 1990s.

Such calamities which disfigure God's earth are a summons, and a judgment. We have not always been agents of God's peace. It is surely a source of discomfort for us to learn that the twentieth century's most celebrated man of peace, Gandhi, was neither a Muslim nor a Christian. And as a European, citizen of a continent which is proud of its monotheistic heritage, I continue to be desolated by the memory of the wars of the past century, which outstripped both in scale and ferocity those of any other continent.

We are called, it is evident, to prove to the world that we are a force for good. The modern crisis of faith is all too often triggered by a sense that religion yields the bitter fruit of enmity and even conflict. Our most urgent task, then, as we seek to recover our place as defenders of human dignity and mutual respect, is to show, in practice, and not only in words, that we can cooperate together for the common good. Natural disasters, seemingly so prominent in our environmentally troubled times, offer an obvious field for common labour, and one follows with delight the progress of the cooperation between CAFOD and Islamic Relief, after the historic Memorandum of Understanding which they signed in 2003, in which they pledge support for each other's activities in emergency work.[9] Islamic Relief and Christian Aid are also, in my own country, sending joint Muslim-Christian teams to areas of southern Africa, in a pilot scheme which holds the promise of further and more systematic cooperation. And at the enormous Cut the Carbon Rally in Birmingham, on August 21, 2007, Christian Aid and several Muslim charities demonstrated the healing power of a public event which announced to the world that its environmental suffering can be healed by interreligious cooperation, pooling energy and resources to tackle a problem that is too large for

[9] www.cafod.org.uk/partnership/other-faiths

the agencies of one faith alone.

The global famine that seems to come ever closer, prompted, perhaps, by the rise in bio-fuel consumption, is already creating lethal competition for scarce resources in many Third World countries. Deaths from hunger are increasingly reported, and small producers too are suffering. In India, figures show that an appalling 166,000 farmers have committed suicide since 1997.[10] Our shared wisdom regarding just distribution, compassion for the needy, the evils of usury, and a political struggle on behalf of the oppressed, should surely be put to use in a joint campaign, in the name of our father Abraham, to defend those who suffer in this way.

This should be particularly our duty and burden. Both Islam and Catholicism are in Europe. But neither should claim a privileged relationship with that continent, for fear of relegating others to a secondary status. Both of our traditions have substantial roots in Asia and Africa. Asia is, in one sense, the privileged continent, the continent of the spirit, as Heaven has made it the birthplace of all the major religions. Today many parts of it thrive, but in others, human dignity is suffering grievously. And in Africa, now a continent shared intimately between Islam and Christianity, we are also called to work together for what we hold in common. Jesus and Muhammad were not only champions of the poor, they lived among the poor, and will surely be resurrected among them. That is a vital aspect of their brotherhood and of ours. If we live in privilege, taking vain pride in our titles and garments, but fail to work with our own hands and hearts for those whose livelihoods are precarious, then we will have betrayed the Abrahamic principle of submission to God's will, which is that we be ready to sacrifice even what is most precious to us, unhesitatingly, with full hearts for God's sake.

[10] Randeep Ramesh, *The Guardian*, 1 March 2008.

The words of the Quran are summoning and reproaching us all:

> Have you seen the one who denies religion?
> It is he who pushes away the orphan,
> And who does not urge the feeding of the poor.
> So woe to those who worship,
> Who are absent-minded in their prayer;
> Those who make a show of themselves,
> And refuse neighbourly assistance.
>
> (Sura 107)

We and You - Let us Meet in God's Love*

by Seyyed Hossein Nasr

بسم الله الرحمن الرحيم

In the Name of God, the All-Good, the Infinitely Merciful and blessings and peace be upon the Prophet Muḥammad and upon all the messengers.

Your Holiness, Eminences, Excellencies, Distinguished Scholars:

It is asserted by the Word of God, which for us Muslims is the Noble Quran, "And God summons to the Abode of Peace," and by Christ (may peace be upon him), who is the Word of God in Christianity and also a prophet of the highest order in Islam, "Blessed are the peacemakers." The goal of attaining peace is thus common between our two religions and we are here precisely with the hope of attaining peace between Christianity and Islam. Furthermore, what can be more important and foundational in the quest for peace than creating peace between our religions—for only from this peace will it be possible to establish peace between peoples and nations, more specifically the Islamic world and the West. Whether we are Christians or Muslims, we are beckoned by our religions to seek peace. As people of religion meeting here at the center of Catholicism, let us then dedicate ourselves to mutual understanding, not as diplomats, but as sincere religious scholars and authorities standing before God and responsible to Him beyond all worldly authority.

* *This is the full text of the paper prepared for the Catholic-Muslim Forum held at the Vatican November 4-6, 2008. An abridged version was delivered to His Holiness and participants on November 6.*

When one ponders the remarkable similarities between Islam and Christianity, one wonders why there has been so much contention between the two religions over the centuries. As Muslims we share with Christians faith in the One God, the God of Abraham, and see in the beginning of the Catholic declaration of belief, *credo in unum deum*, the deepest confirmation of the first *shahādah* or testimony of our religion, namely *lā ilāha illa 'Llāh* (there is no divinity but God), which we consider to be foundational not only to our religion, but to every authentic religion. Our religion and yours share, therefore, the same foundation and basis despite differences among us in the interpretation of the doctrine of *tawḥīd*, or unity, that is so central not only to Islam but also to Christianity since the doctrine of the Trinity certainly does not negate Divine Unity in mainstream Christian theology.

Moreover, for us God is the Creator and Sustainer of the universe, at once Transcendent and Immanent, as He is for you. Over the many centuries of our history men and women of our two communities have stood in awe before the majesty of God as Transcendent and felt His closeness as the Immanent, for as the Noble Quran asserts God is closer to us than our jugular vein. And there have been those in our two communities who have smelled the perfume of Divine Proximity, have become immersed in the Ocean of Oneness and been blessed by the beatific vision of God.

For both of us God has a personal dimension and we can address Him as the "Thou" to whom we both pray. For Muslims as well as Christians God is both Merciful and Just and the harmonization of these two apparently contradictory Qualities has been the subject of countless studies by both your theologians and ours. And of course we both associate God with love with different interpretations of this central Divine Quality in our two religions. Christians speak of the love of God and some view Islam as lacking in emphasizing this Quality. Muslims would respond that God being infinite, surely His love for His creation could not have become exhausted by the advent of Christianity. Some of that love must in fact have remained to be manifested in Islam and we, no less than Christians, live the life of faith in the glow of Divine Love. That is why one of the greatest spiritual masters of Islam, Jalal al-Din Rumi, identified God with the Beloved, as did so many other Sufis, and could utter in a poem:

Hail to Thee O our Love with goodly passion,
O physician of all our ailments,
O remedy of our pride and honor,
O Thou our Plato and Galen besides.

Both you and we believe that God has created the human soul which is immortal and reject all those views that consider man as a clever machine brought about through accidental and haphazard biological events. We both associate human dignity with men's and women's eternal soul. Consequently we both emphasize the ethical character of human life and believe that having been given free will to act, we are responsible to God for our earthly actions. Our theologians may have debated about free will and determinism for many centuries but both religions have always insisted upon morality and the ethical nature of human actions with consequences beyond the grave. We all affirm the reality of good and evil and their basic distinction, without which belief in ethical action and its effect upon our immortal soul would be meaningless. And our ethical norms are in fact similar in so many ways. That is why we both seek to avoid what classical Catholic theology calls the seven deadly sins. That is why on the social plane we both emphasize the importance of the family and on the individual level the crucial significance of sexual ethics, which, although dealing primarily with the individual, has such a major impact upon society at large.

For both you and us it is our common eschatological beliefs, in their general principles and not details, that provide the framework for the religious understanding of human actions and their consequences upon our souls. We all believe in the reality of posthumous states, in various paradises, infernos and at least in the case of Catholic Christianity the purgatories. All of us expect to meet God and rely on His mercy and forgiveness. We even have fairly similar historical eschatologies with of course some differences, but in any case we both expect the second coming of Christ, who is at once the center of Christianity and such a major figure in the Islamic religious universe.

We Muslims and Christians, like followers of other religions, pray, and although the external forms are different, there are remarkable similarities in our prayers. Some of us say "O God forgive us our sins" and others *astaghfiru'Llāh*, that is, "I ask forgiveness of God." The life of the pious person, whether Christian or Muslim, is intertwined with prayer and both religions are witness to a vast spectrum of prayers from the simple petition to God for some need or want to the prayer of the heart, of the saints who only want "Thy will be done" or "I want not to want."

Also over the centuries both Christians and Muslims have made pilgrimage and many continue to do so, Christians to such places as St. James of Compostella, Lourdes, and in earlier Christian history Canterbury, and Muslims primarily to Makkah and Madinah but also many other sites including Jerusalem which has been shared by both Muslims and Christians as a site of pilgrimage. Indeed, the external forms are different but how similar was and is the inner experience of pilgrimage in our two religions!

"How precious is the gift of faith!" Such an assertion can be made equally by a Christian and a Muslim. Whether one speaks of *fides* or *īmān*, one is dealing with a most profound reality shared by Muslims and Christians alike. Moreover, both religious communities have encountered the relative significance of faith and works in their religious life. Remarkably enough every theological position taken in Christianity as a whole on the question of the relation and relative significance of faith and works has its equivalence *mutatis mutandis* in Islam.

Such is also true of the question of free will and determinism. Islamic thought is not confined to Ash'arism nor Christianity to Calvinism. It is false to assert that Islam is fatalistic and deterministic while Christianity is based on free will. In reality the rich theological and philosophical schools of both religions present a full spectrum of views on this crucial subject. Nor could this have been otherwise, for the followers of both religions experience in an immediate way, as do all human beings, their freedom to act. Yet along with Jews, they stand before the God of Abraham whose Will reigns supreme.

How strange that Muslims have been accused of being opposed to reason while it was a Muslim philosopher and jurist, Ibn Rushd or Averroes, who is considered to have been the single most important figure in the introduction of rationalist arguments into medieval Christian theology. The reality of the matter is that both Christians and Muslims have presented and held many diverse views concerning the relation between reason and faith or reason and revelation and practically every view in one religion finds its counterpart in the other, except that of course Islam did not encounter Enlightenment rationalism in the 18th century and did not surrender to its tenets as did certain strands of Christianity. In any case, persons of faith in both religions stand before the Majesty of God and His all-powerful Will as well as all-encompassing knowledge. And among them those who have had philosophical and theological tendencies have had to ponder over the relation between reason and revelation and have come often to similar conclusions. It is true that in Christianity God is a mystery hidden from man and in Islam it is not He who is hidden and a mystery but man who is hidden from God. And yet, the question of the relation between reason and faith, far from being a source of contention between the two religions, is a source of common accord if one considers the full spectrum of the traditional theologies and philosophies of Christianity and Islam.

Both religions having been sent by God to lead human beings back to Him, Christianity and Islam are channels of grace and make possible not only salvation but also the experience of sanctity as well as the attainment of inner illumination. The pious life of both religions has, through the centuries, been involved with the reality of sanctity in one way or another despite the eclipse of this dimension of religious life in recent times in both religions, in Western Christianity due to the advent of secularism and in Islam as a result of the rise of what has now come to be known as "fundamentalism." One can only ask what the relation between Christianity and Islam would be if saints, men and women whose being are rooted in God, represented each religion in dialogue. In any case, the reality of sanctity as well as spiritual leadership, whether associated with an *imām* or a superior of a Catholic order are shared between us. In Shi'ism and certain schools of Sunnism, we speak of *walāyah* which means spiritual power, sanctity and inner guidance. Surely Christians would find in this concept and reality deep similarities to their own doctrines.

It is also important to recall that both Islam and Christianity have created major civilizations with their own social structures, sciences, philosophies, arts, etc. Both have created sacred architecture of the highest order whether it be Chartres or the Mezquita in Cordova. Both have produced most outstanding examples of literature imbued with the values of the religions in question. Outward forms differ but the inner meanings of traditional Islamic and Christian arts and sciences—and not the humanistic and modernistic distortions of the traditional norms—are very close and should be a means of bringing the two religions closer together.

Speaking of Christian and Islamic civilizations, it must be noted that the name of both religions has been associated with violence in certain periods of their history. To associate only Islam with violence is to overlook the fact that over the centuries many more Muslims have been killed by Christians than Christians by Muslims. If there is more violence today carried out in the name of Islam than of Christianity, that is not due to the support of violence by one religion and opposition to violence by the other, but rather the result of the relative strength of each religion today. If Christianity in the West is no longer associated with violence, it is because of the weakening of Christianity before the onslaught of secularism. One could hardly imagine calling French or British soldiers to war these days in the name of Christianity, in contrast to older days from the Crusades to the destruction of natives in the Americas when Christianity being strong, was used oftentimes by political forces to legitimize wars and violence. To associate Islam simply with violence and Christianity with non-violence is to make virtue out of necessity. The task to confront and oppose violence in all its forms is in fact a task in whose realization both Muslims and Christians must work hand in hand.

When we ponder over what unites us, we are confronted with the issue of human dignity. The views of the two religions are indeed close in this crucial matter. Traditional and classical Christianity and Islam both believe in human dignity because as both religions have asserted "God has created man in His image" whatever different meanings we attach to the word "image." Furthermore, God has breathed into us His Spirit and that is the origin of human dignity we both accept and the source of human rights. To base human rights and freedoms on humanistic, evolutionary and secularist conceptions of man is merely to espouse a position that is based on sheer sentimentality bereft of any theological foundation and opposed by serious theological thought, both Islamic and Christian.

These are but a few of the realities shared by us and you. Why then has there been such confrontation and opposition between Christianity and Islam? One must consider first of all the fact that Islam appeared after Christianity and from the dawn of Islam Muslims have had respect for Christianity as a revealed religion, and have protected the Christians living among them and as they continue to in sizeable numbers in several Islamic countries. In contrast Christianity preceded Islam and its mainstream religious thought did not accept and for the most part does not accept even now Islam as an authentic religion revealed by God and given the power to bring about salvation to its followers. There are also formal differences many of which were divinely ordained in order to keep the two religions distinct. Had not those providential distinctions existed, we would not be speaking to each other as followers of two religions today, both of which have not only survived but possess a global presence to this day, a situation surely willed by God for those of us who accept God as the Almighty whose Will rules supreme. Let us then turn to some of those differences.

Islam emphasizes Divine Unity which being Absolute cannot enter into any relation, for that would imply relativity; hence the Islamic rejection of the Trinitarian doctrine and the possibility of Divine Sonship. Christianity on the contrary emphasizes the Triune nature of God while like Islam accepting His Oneness. Likewise, the two religions differ in their account of the end of the life of Christ who plays such an important spiritual role in the Islamic religious universe as well as being the heart and center of Christianity. The question between the two religions that remains is the following: was Christ crucified or not? And the answer to this crucial question is not the same as far as Islam and Christianity are concerned.

On the social plane, Islam emphasizes the centrality of the Divine Law (*al-Sharī'ah*) whose main sources are the Noble Quran and the *Sunnah* or wonts of the Prophet of Islam while for Christianity the law of Christ is a spiritual law and in everyday affairs Christianity incorporated much of Roman Law and later Germanic common law. The result is different views concerning the significance of laws that govern human society. Likewise, on the social plane Christianity preached giving unto God what is God's and unto Caesar what is Caesar's. This meant the complete separation of spiritual and temporal authority, although in practice after Constantine the two became intertwined resulting practically in a situation not very different from that of Islam which has never accepted the separation of the domains of God and Caesar. Today both religions struggle with this question but for different reasons.

When we come to the organization of religion we again detect important differences. In Catholic Christianity there is the ordained priesthood and only priests can perform certain ritual actions, especially the consecration of the Eucharist. In Islam every man is a priest and there is no religious hierarchy as we find in Christianity in general and Catholicism in particular. Even the hierarchy found in Shi'ism is not the same as that found in Catholicism and a Shi'ite, like his Sunni brothers, is a priest in being able to conduct all the rites of the religion from performing or leading the daily canonical prayers to leading the prayer for the dead.

What or who is the Divine Word? To this question a Christian would answer Christ and a Muslim the Noble Quran, although in certain schools of Islamic thought each prophet including Jesus has been identified with an aspect of the Divine Word. In any case, for Christians the body of Christ is the "container" of the Word, while for Islam it is the Quranic Arabic language which, as the result of the Islamic revelation, became by God's Will the sacred language of Islam and the "container" of God's Word. Christianity has had many liturgical languages, including, besides Latin, Aramaic, Greek, Russian, Slavonic and even Arabic which is thus the sacred language of Islam as well as the liturgical language of Arab Christians. This different understanding of the role of language in religious rites has had many significant consequences. Not only Arabs, but all Muslims, whether Malay, Indo-Pakistani, Persian, Turk or African, all having mother tongues other than Arabic, pray five times a day in Arabic, whereas in the West after nearly two millennia of the use of the beautiful Latin liturgy, it was put aside in favor of vernacular languages after Vatican II.

Many have said that for Christianity, Islamic teachings have been too close for comfort and there is what one might call family enmity towards Islam that Christianity has not had towards other religions, the case of Judaism being an exceptional one. Yes, Christians read in the Holy Bible about Noah, Abraham and Moses, all of whom along with many other prophets are also mentioned in the Noble Quran. Christians, especially Catholic and Orthodox, venerate the Virgin Mary and so do Muslims. For Christians, Jesus is the Son of God, who was born miraculously from a virgin mother and who performed of many miracles. For Muslims he is not the son of God but one of the foremost prophets dedicated to spiritual guidance, the prophet of inwardness, born miraculously of a virgin mother. Yes, Muslims also venerate Mary, the only woman after whom a chapter of the Quran is named. Moreover, they not only accept the virginal birth of Jesus as do Christians, but also affirm his performance of miracles. Despite differences, the similarities are great enough to have aroused suspicion and special enmity among many Christians against Islam even after the political threat of Islam to Europe had disappeared.

There are also significant differences between Islam and Christianity due to their very different encounters with modernism and secularism. Obviously in dealing with Christianity today, we Muslims are not confronted with St. Thomas Aquinas, Dante, and the builders of the Cologne Cathedral, however real these dimensions of traditional Western Christianity might still be. Rather, we face a Christianity that bears the deep wounds of five centuries of battle with forces opposed to religion, from the secular humanism and skepticism of the Renaissance to the materialism associated with the 17th century Scientific Revolution and the subsequent secularization of the cosmos to the rationalism of the Age of Enlightenment, to the historicism and evolutionism of the 19th century to the current post-modern critique of religious texts and the virulent atheistic attacks being made recently in the West against religion as such. Western Christianity has had to face such figures as Montaigne, Bayle, Feuerbach, Marx and Freud, all of whom were products of the West and not from a land far away as has been the case of Islam in its confrontation with such figures. Islam, moreover, did not experience various phases of modernism in a gradual manner as did Western Christianity, but experienced it rapidly and in quick order. Of course there are those in the West who claim that the problem is precisely that Islam did not experience in depth modernism and especially the Enlightenment to which Muslims would respond, thank God that this did not happen to us. Otherwise the number of Muslim worshippers performing the Friday prayers at the Sultan Hasan Mosque in Cairo would be the same as the number of Christians participating in the Mass on a Sunday at the St. Sulpice Church in Paris.

In seeking to come together we must be fully aware of the differences created by the advent of modernism. Western Christianity has fought against but also in many cases surrendered to the foe as we see in the abandonment of the cosmos to a secularist science or the adoption of certain Marxist themes in some of the currents of liberation theology. As for Islam, its encounter with modernism has been confined to a short period. Within the span of a century Muslims have had to face the challenges of five centuries of European anti-religious thought. Their reaction has, therefore, been different from that of Western Christianity. Islam's encounter with modernism has not produced an army of influential secularist thinkers, nor a strong wave against religion as we see in modern European history. But there have been severe reactions, sometimes unfortunately violent, to modernism throughout the Islamic world recently, resulting in what is called problematically in the West fundamentalism which, however, also has its equivalents in both Judaism and Christianity not to speak of Hinduism.

Let us understand the roots of our differences not only as based in scripture and tradition, but also as resulting from our very different experiences of modernism and secularism. Simple criticism of the other without understanding and empathy cannot bring accord despite all the elements common between Islam and Christianity to which some reference has already been made. We are situated in the same boat floating over very dangerous waters. The vilification of the other through accentuation of differences without deeper understanding of causes of these differences and disregard for all that unites us, especially the love of God and the neighbor, cannot but lead to our own perdition.

Forgetting and casting aside the remarkable accord on so many basic doctrines and values and exaggerating differences used often to bring about purposefully discord and opposition have characterized much of the history of relations between our two religions. As we now all stand at the edge of a precipice it is time to turn a new page and seek to come together in the bosom of Divine Love. Of course our coming together does not and should not mean the destruction of divinely ordained formal structures of each religion. You and us: we must in fact be able to continue our distinct religious lives without constant threat of the destruction of our faith from the other side before even embarking upon dialogue. That is why we Muslims oppose aggressive proselytizing which seeks to reward conversion with worldly advantages. We wish to preserve our religion, as do the Jews, who in 1988 passed a law in Israel banning religious proselytizing, as would

Christians if they were placed in our situation. To be friends requires that we first exist as ourselves. The other must be respected as the other, not as potential material for conversion from the category of otherness. Yes, both Christianity and Islam envisage for themselves a universal message, but if we are to live together in peace, we cannot try to destroy the religious identity of the other at all costs, imposing what we consider to be our right on the other, and disregarding his right for self-preservation.

Our attitudes in this matter as in so many others will change if we realize not only theoretically, but also concretely, that we belong to the same family of religions, worshipping the same God. The great tragedies of the 20th century have helped to expand the usage of the term "Judeo-Christian." It is now time to realize that we have to speak of "Judeo-Christian-Islamic" if we are to be honest, and also reverential towards Abraham, who is the father of monotheism. It was God's Will that the Abrahamic tradition should be comprised of the three religions of Judaism, Christianity and Islam. You cannot sever bonds that have been forged by God. If we are to accept in our hearts, and not only diplomatically, that we are members of the same religious family (seen in the positive sense of family based on accord and not discord), then we must discourse with each other as family members and respect each other in every way without hatred and above the fray of family feuds. Our dialogues must not be based on suspicion, hidden agendas and duplicity, but on sincerity and honesty, which are so much needed in our world. We are not each other's enemies, but members of the same divinely ordained family. Therefore, we should not try to destroy each other, but seek to vie with each other in goodness, as the Noble Quran asserts.

One might understand that a thousand years ago, when we both lived in a world impregnated by faith, some Christians might have called Muslims their enemies, and vice versa, although even then many Christians and Muslims lived as friends as can be seen in the long history of Christian communities in the Islamic world. In any case, we no longer live in a traditional world of faith and are confronting other enemies. We live in a secularist world in which religions are each other's best friends. In any case, today our enemy, which in fact is common between us, is the materialistic, hedonistic, nihilistic and God-negating world-view that is so wide-spread, the world-view that negates the spiritual nature of humanity, denies the sacred and the transcendent, and seeks to shatter our hopes for a blessed life everlasting. We have much to offer to each other in the central battle between truth and falsehood. But the offer can only be accepted if we first recognize each other as friends and not as enemies.

In this effort to reorient ourselves toward each other, all of us, Christian and Muslim alike, can play a role. But there is no doubt that the main responsibility lies on the shoulders of religious leaders, thinkers and scholars, those whom we call *'ulamā'* in Islam. Those who are guides and trailblazers in religious matters must come forward and seek to bring about understanding to those in their own communities who hearken to their call. They should bring about further knowledge about the other whom they should present as friend, not enemy, to be loved and not vilified. And surely the carrying out of such a task on our part is one that is not always easy. It requires—besides the necessary knowledge—selflessness, honesty and truthfulness in conjunction with love and compassion.

We as Muslims from different schools of Islamic thought and countries have come together to extend to you our hand of friendship, seeking to meet you in God's love, beyond all our theological differences and memories of historical confrontations. Surely we, who respect and love Christ as you do, can meet and come together under the banner of what he has stated to be the two supreme commandments: to love God and to love the neighbor. We can also seek to extend, often in harmony with each other, the border of the definition of neighbor to include not only you and us but the whole of humanity, and even beyond that the rest of God's creation. As the Holy Bible asserts, "With God, all things are possible." We submit to Him, and ask for His help and affirmation in carrying out this momentous task of meeting with you in friendship and peace under the banner of that common word that unites us. There can be no more blessed act in our times than the creation of deep accord between God's religions, especially the two religions that have the largest numbers of followers in the world, namely Christianity and Islam. Indeed, God summons us to the Abode of Peace, and blessed are the peace-makers.

Address of His Holiness Benedict XVI To Participants in the Seminar Organized by the "Catholic-Muslim Forum"

Clementine Hall
Thursday, 6 November 2008

Dear Friends,

I am pleased to receive you this morning and I greet all of you most cordially. I thank especially Cardinal Jean-Louis Tauran as well as Shaykh Mustafa Ceri and Dr. Seyyed Hossein Nasr for their words. Our meeting takes place at the conclusion of the important Seminar organized by the "Catholic-Muslim Forum" established between the Pontifical Council for Interreligious Dialogue and representatives of the 138 Muslim leaders who signed the Open Letter to Christian leaders of 13 October 2007. This gathering is a clear sign of our mutual esteem and our desire to listen respectfully to one another. I can assure you that I have prayerfully followed the progress of your meeting, conscious that it represents one more step along the way towards greater understanding between Muslims and Christians within the framework of other regular encounters which the Holy See promotes with various Muslim groups. The Open Letter *A Common Word between Us and You* has received numerous responses, and has given rise to dialogue, specific initiatives and meetings, aimed at helping us to know one another more deeply and to grow in esteem for our shared values. The great interest which the present Seminar has awakened is an incentive for us to ensure that the reflections and the positive developments which emerge from Muslim-Christian dialogue are not limited to a small group of experts and scholars, but are passed on as a precious legacy to be placed at the service of all, to bear fruit in the way we live each day.

The theme which you have chosen for your meeting—"Love of God, Love of Neighbour: The Dignity of the Human Person and Mutual Respect"—is particularly significant. It was taken from the Open Letter, which presents love of God and love of neighbour as the heart of Islam and Christianity alike. This theme highlights even more clearly the theological and spiritual foundations of a central teaching of our respective religions.

The Christian tradition proclaims that God is Love (cf. 1 Jn 4:16). It was out of love that he created the whole universe, and by his love he becomes present in human history. The love of God became visible, manifested fully and definitively in Jesus Christ. He thus came down to meet man and, while remaining God, took on our nature. He gave himself in order to restore full dignity to each person and to bring us salvation. How could we ever explain the mystery of the incarnation and the redemption except by Love? This infinite and eternal love enables us to respond by giving all our love in return: love for God and love for neighbour. This truth, which we consider foundational, was what I wished to emphasize in my first Encyclical, *Deus Caritas Est*, since this is a central teaching of the Christian faith. Our calling and mission is to share freely with others the love which God lavishes upon us without any merit of our own.

I am well aware that Muslims and Christians have different approaches in matters regarding God. Yet we can and must be worshippers of the one God who created us and is concerned about each person in every corner of the world. Together we must show, by our mutual respect and solidarity, that we consider ourselves members of one family: the family that God has loved and gathered together from the creation of the world to the end of human history.

I was pleased to learn that you were able at this meeting to adopt a common position on the need to worship God totally and to love our fellow men and women disinterestedly, especially those in distress and need. God calls us to work together on behalf of the victims of disease, hunger, poverty, injustice and violence. For Christians, the love of God is inseparably bound to the love of our brothers and sisters, of all men and women, without distinction of race and culture. As Saint John writes: "Those who say, 'I love God,' and hate their brothers or sisters are liars; for those who do not love a brother or sister whom they have seen, cannot love God whom they have not seen" (1 Jn 4:20).

The Muslim tradition is also quite clear in encouraging practical commitment in serving the most needy, and readily recalls the "Golden Rule" in its own version: your faith will not be perfect, unless you do unto others that which you wish for yourselves. We should thus work together in promoting genuine respect for the dignity of the human person and fundamental human rights, even though our anthropological visions and our theologies justify this in different ways. There is a great and vast field in which we can act together in defending and promoting the moral values which are part of our common heritage. Only by starting with the recognition of the centrality of the person and the dignity of each human being, respecting and defending life which is the gift of God, and is thus sacred for Christians and for Muslims alike—only on the basis of this recognition, can we find a common ground for building a more fraternal world, a world in which confrontations and differences are peacefully settled, and the devastating power of ideologies is neutralized.

My hope, once again, is that these fundamental human rights will be protected for all people everywhere. Political and religious leaders have the duty of ensuring the free exercise of these rights in full respect for each individual's freedom of conscience and freedom of religion. The discrimination and violence which even today religious people experience throughout the world, and the often violent persecutions to which they are subject, represent unacceptable and unjustifiable acts, all the more grave and deplorable when they are carried out in the name of God. God's name can only be a name of peace and fraternity, justice and love. We are challenged to demonstrate, by our words and above all by our deeds, that the message of our religions is unfailingly a message of harmony and mutual understanding. It is essential that we do so, lest we weaken the credibility and the effectiveness not only of our dialogue, but also of our religions themselves.

I pray that the "Catholic-Muslim Forum," now confidently taking its first steps, can become ever more a space for dialogue, and assist us in treading together the path to an ever fuller knowledge of Truth. The present meeting is also a privileged occasion for committing ourselves to a more heartfelt quest for love of God and love of neighbour, the indispensable condition for offering the men and women of our time an authentic service of reconciliation and peace.

Dear friends, let us unite our efforts, animated by good will, in order to overcome all misunderstanding and disagreements. Let us resolve to overcome past prejudices and to correct the often distorted images of the other which even today can create difficulties in our relations; let us work with one another to educate all people, especially the young, to build a common future. May God sustain us in our good intentions, and enable our communities to live consistently the truth of love, which constitutes the heart of the religious man, and is the basis of respect for the dignity of each person. May God, the merciful and compassionate One, assist us in this challenging mission, protect us, bless us and enlighten us always with the power of his love.

First Seminar of the Catholic-Muslim Forum
Rome, 4-6 November 2008

Final Declaration

The Catholic-Muslim Forum was formed by the Pontifical Council for Interreligious Dialogue and a delegation of the 138 Muslim signatories of the open letter called *A Common Word*, in the light of the same document and the response of His Holiness Benedict XVI through his Secretary of State, Cardinal Tarcisio Bertone. Its first Seminar was held in Rome from 4-6 November 2008. Twenty-four participants and five advisors from each religion took part in the meeting. The theme of the Seminar was "Love of God, Love of Neighbour".

The discussion, conducted in a warm and convivial spirit, focused on two great themes: "Theological and Spiritual Foundations" and "Human Dignity and Mutual Respect". Points of similarity and of diversity emerged, reflecting the distinctive specific genius of the two religions.

1. For Christians the source and example of love of God and neighbour is the love of Christ for his Father, for humanity and for each person. "God is Love" (1 Jn 4,16) and "God so loved the world that He gave his only Son so that whoever believes in him shall not perish but have eternal life" (Jn 3,16). God's love is placed in the human heart through the Holy Spirit. It is God who first loves us thereby enabling us to love Him in return. Love does not harm one's neighbour but rather seeks to do to the other what one would want done to oneself (Cf. 1 Cor 13, 4-7). Love is the foundation and sum of all the commandments (Cf. Gal 5, 14). Love of neighbour cannot be separated from love of God, because it is an expression of our love for

God. This is the new commandment, "Love one another as I have loved you." (Jn 15, 12) Grounded in Christ's sacrificial love, Christian love is forgiving and excludes no one; it therefore also includes one's enemies. It should be not just words but deeds (Cf. 1 Jn, 4, 18). This is the sign of its genuineness.

For Muslims, as set out in *A Common Word*, love is a timeless transcendent power which guides and transforms human mutual regard. This love, as indicated by the Holy and Beloved Prophet Muhammad, is prior to the human love for the One True God. A *hadith* indicates that God's loving compassion for humanity is even greater than that of a mother for her child (Muslim, Bab al-Tawba: 21); it therefore exists before and independently of the human response to the One who is "The Loving". So immense is this love and compassion that God has intervened to guide and save humanity in a perfect way many times and in many places, by sending prophets and scriptures. The last of these books, the Quran, portrays a world of signs, a marvelous cosmos of Divine artistry, which calls forth our utter love and devotion, so that "those who have faith, have most love of God" (2:165), and "those that believe, and do good works, the Merciful shall engender love among them." (19:96) In a *hadith* we read that "Not one of you has faith until he loves for his neighbour what he loves for himself" (Bukhari, Bab al-Iman: 13).

2. Human life is a most precious gift of God to each person. It should therefore be preserved and honoured in all its stages.

3. Human dignity is derived from the fact that every human person is created by a loving God, and has been endowed with the gifts of reason and free will, and therefore enabled to love God and others. On the firm basis of these principles, the person requires the respect of his or her original dignity and his or her human vocation. Therefore, he or she is entitled to full recognition of his or her identity and freedom by individuals, communities and governments, supported by civil legislation that assures equal rights and full citizenship.

4. We affirm that God's creation of humanity has two great aspects: the male and the female human person, and we commit ourselves jointly to ensuring that human dignity and respect are extended on an equal basis to both men and women.

5. Genuine love of neighbour implies respect of the person and her or his choices in matters of conscience and religion. It includes the right of individuals and communities to practice their religion in private and public.

6. Religious minorities are entitled to be respected in their own religious convictions and practices. They are also entitled to their own places of worship, and their founding figures and symbols they consider sacred should not be subject to any form of mockery or ridicule.

7. As Catholic and Muslim believers, we are aware of the summons and imperative to bear witness to the transcendent dimension of life, through a spirituality nourished by prayer, in a world which is becoming more and more secularized and materialistic.

8. We affirm that no religion and its followers should be excluded from society. Each should be able to make its indispensable contribution to the good of society, especially in service to the most needy.

9. We recognize that God's creation in its plurality of cultures, civilizations, languages and peoples is a source of richness and should therefore never become a cause of tension and conflict.

10. We are convinced that Catholics and Muslims have the duty to provide a sound education in human, civic, religious and moral values for their respective members and to promote accurate information about each other's religions.

11. We profess that Catholics and Muslims are called to be instruments of love and harmony among believers, and for humanity as a whole, renouncing any oppression, aggressive violence and terrorism, especially that committed in

the name of religion, and upholding the principle of justice for all.

12. We call upon believers to work for an ethical financial system in which the regulatory mechanisms consider the situation of the poor and disadvantaged, both as individuals, and as indebted nations. We call upon the privileged of the world to consider the plight of those afflicted most severely by the current crisis in food production and distribution, and ask religious believers of all denominations and all people of good will to work together to alleviate the suffering of the hungry, and to eliminate its causes.

13. Young people are the future of religious communities and of societies as a whole. Increasingly, they will be living in multicultural and multi-religious societies. It is essential that they be well formed in their own religious traditions and well informed about other cultures and religions.

14. We have agreed to explore the possibility of establishing a permanent Catholic-Muslim committee to coordinate responses to conflicts and other emergency situations.

15. We look forward to the second Seminar of the Catholic-Muslim Forum to be convened in approximately two years in a Muslim-majority country yet to be determined.

All participants felt gratitude to God for the gift of their time together and for an enriching exchange.

بسم الله الرحمن الرحيم

Bismi'Llāh al-Raḥmān al-Raḥīm
wa'l-Ṣalātu wa'l-Salāmu 'alā'l-Nabī al-'Arabī al-Hāshimī
al-Amīn, Khātim al-Anbiyā' wa'l-Mursalīn

Address to H.H. Pope Benedict XVI at the King Hussein Mosque, Amman, Jordan

By H.R.H. Prince Ghazi bin Muhammad bin Talal

Al-Salaam 'Aleikum,
Pax Vobis,

On the occasion of this historic visit to the King Hussein bin Talal Mosque here in Amman, Jordan, I bid Your Holiness Pope Benedict XVI welcome in four ways.

First, as a *Muslim*, I bid Your Holiness welcome today, as we understand this visit to be a deliberate gesture of goodwill and mutual respect from the Supreme Spiritual Leader and Pontiff of the largest denomination of the world's largest religion to the world's second largest religion. Indeed, Christians and Muslims together make up over 55% of the world's population and so it is especially significant that this is only the third time in history a reigning Pope has visited a mosque; the first being by Your Holiness's much beloved predecessor Pope John Paul II to the historical Umayyad Mosque in Damascus (which contains the remains of John the Baptist [may peace be upon him]) in 2001, and the second being by Your Holiness to the Magnificent Blue Mosque of Sultan Ahmed in Istanbul in 2006. The beautiful

Saturday May 9, 2009 CE, 14th Jamada Al-Uwla, 1430 AH

King Hussein Mosque here in Amman, Jordan is Jordan's State Mosque and it was built and personally supervised by His Majesty King Abdullah II in loving honour of his late father, Jordan's great King Hussein (may God have mercy on his soul). Thus, this is the first time in history that a Pope has ever visited a *new* mosque. Hence we see in this visit a clear message of the necessity of interfaith harmony and mutual respect in the *contemporary* world, as well as concrete proof of the willingness of Your Holiness to personally take a leading role in this. This gesture is all the more remarkable given the fact that this visit to Jordan by Your Holiness is primarily a spiritual pilgrimage to the Christian Holy Land (and in particular to the site of the Baptism of Jesus Christ [may peace be upon him] by John the Baptist [peace be upon him] at "Bethany beyond the Jordan" (John 1:28 and John 3:26), and yet Your Holiness has made time in your intense and tiring schedule—tiring for a man of any age—for this visit to the King Hussein Mosque in order to honour Muslims.

I must also thank Your Holiness for the "regret" you expressed after the Regensburg lecture of September 13th 2006 for the hurt caused by this lecture to Muslims. Of course, Muslims know that nothing said or done in this world can harm the Prophet (may peace and blessings be upon him), who, as his last words attested, is with the Highest Companion—God Himself—in Paradise, but Muslims were nevertheless hurt because of their love for the Prophet (may peace and blessings be upon him), who is, as God says in the Holy Quran, "closer to the believers than their own selves" (*Al-Ahzab*, 33:6). Hence, Muslims also especially appreciated the clarification by the Vatican that what was said in the Regensburg lecture did not reflect Your Holiness's own opinion, but rather was simply a citation in an academic lecture.

It hardly needs to be said, moreover, that the Prophet Muhammad (may peace and blessings be upon him) whom Muslims love, emulate and know as a living reality and spiritual presence, *is completely and entirely different* from the historical depictions of him in the West since St. John of Damascus. These distorted depictions by those who either do not know Arabic or the Holy Quran and the *Ḥadīth*, or who do not understand the historical and cultural context of the Prophet's life—and thus misunderstand and misconstrue the spiritual motives and intentions behind many of the Prophet's (may peace and blessings be upon him) actions and words—are unfortunately responsible for much historical and cultural tension between Christians and Muslims. It is thus incumbent on Muslims to explain the Prophet's example (may peace and blessings be upon him) above all with deeds of virtue, charity, piety and goodwill; recalling that the Prophet himself (may peace and blessings be upon him) was of an "exalted standard of character" (*Al-Qalam*, 68:4). For God says in the Holy Quran:

> Verily ye have in the Messenger of God a beautiful pattern of conduct for whosoever hopes in God and the Last Day, and remembereth God much. (*Al-Ahzab*, 33:21)

Finally, I must also thank Your Holiness for many other friendly gestures and kindly actions towards Muslims since your ascension in 2005—including graciously receiving both H.M. King Abdullah II bin Al-Hussein of Jordan in 2005 and H.M. King AbdAllah bin Abd Al-Aziz of Saudi Arabia, the Custodian of the Two Holy Places in 2008—and especially for your warm reception of the historical "*A Common Word Between Us and You*" Open Letter of October 13th 2007, by 138 leading international Muslim scholars (whose numbers continue increasing to this day). It was as a result of this initiative—which, based on the Holy Qur'an and the Bible, recognised the primacy of the Love of God and Love of the Neighbour in both Christianity and Islam—that the Vatican under your personal guidance held the first seminar of the International Muslim Catholic forum from November the 4th – 6th 2008. We will be shortly *Deo Volente* following up with H.E. the very able Cardinal Tauran the work initiated by this meeting, but for now, I would like to cite and echo your words from the speech your Holiness gave on the occasion of the end of the First Seminar:

> The theme which you have chosen for your meeting—"Love of God, Love of Neighbour: the Dignity of the Human Person and Mutual Respect"—is particularly significant. It was taken from the Open Letter, which presents love of God and love of the neighbour as the heart of Islam and Christianity alike. This theme highlights even more clearly the theological and spiritual foundations of a central teaching of our respective religions. ....
>
> I am well aware that Muslims and Christians have different approaches in matters regarding God. Yet we can and must be worshippers of the One God who created us and is concerned about each person in every corner of the world. ....

> There is a great and vast field in which we can act together in defending and promoting the moral values which are part of our common heritage....

Now I cannot help but remember God's words in the Holy Quran:

> Yet they are not all alike; some of the People of the Scripture are a community upright, who recite God's verses in the watches of the night, prostrating themselves. / They believe in God and in the Last Day, enjoining decency and forbidding indecency, vying with one another in good works; those are of the righteous. / And whatever good they do, they shall not be denied it, and God knows the God-fearing. (*Aal-'Imran*, 3:113-115)

And:

> ...[A]nd you will truly find the nearest of them in love to those who believe to be those who say "Verily, we are Christians"; that is because some of them are priests and monks, and because they are not proud. (*Al-Maida,* 5:82)

Second, as a *Hashemite*, and a descendant of the Prophet Muhammad (may peace and blessings be upon him), I also bid Your Holiness welcome to this mosque in Jordan, remembering that the Prophet (may peace and blessings be upon him) welcomed his Christian neighbours from Najran to Medina and invited them to pray in his own Mosque, which they did, in harmony, without either side compromising their own spiritual beliefs. This, too, is an invaluable message which the world desperately needs to remember.

Third, as an *Arab*—a direct descendant of Ishmael (peace be upon him) of whom the Bible says God would make him "a great nation" (Genesis, 21:18) and that God "was with" him (Genesis, 21:20)—I bid Your Holiness welcome. One of the cardinal virtues of the Arabs—whom traditionally have survived in some of the hottest and most inhospitable climates in the world—is *hospitality*. Hospitality is born of generosity and it recognises the needs of the neighbour and considers those who are far or who come from afar as neighbours, and indeed this virtue is confirmed by God in the Holy Qur'an with the words:

> And worship God, and associate nothing with Him. Be kind to parents, and near kindred, and to orphans, and to the needy, and to the neighbour who is near, and to the neighbour who is a stranger, and to the friend at your side, and to the wayfarer, and to what your right hands possess. Surely God loves not the conceited, and the boastful. (*Al-Nisa*, 4:36)

Arab hospitality means not only loving to give and help, but also being generous of spirit and thus appreciative. In 2000, during the late Pope John Paul II's visit to Jordan, I was working with the Jordanian Tribes, and some tribesmen were saying they really liked the late Pope. Someone asked them why they liked him, since he was a Christian and they were Muslims. They smiled and said: "because he visited us!", and of course the late Pope John Paul II, like yourself could have easily just gone to Israel and Palestine, but instead chose to start his pilgrimage with a visit to us here in Jordan, which we appreciate.

Fourth and finally, as a *Jordanian*, I bid Your Holiness welcome. In Jordan, everyone is equal before the law regardless of religion, race, origin or gender, and those who work in the government are responsible to do their utmost to care for everyone in the country with compassion and with justice. This was the personal example and message of the late King Hussein who over his long reign of forty-seven years felt for everyone in the country as he did for his own children. It is also the message of his son, H.M. King Abdullah II, who accordingly has made it the singular goal of his life and reign to make the life of every Jordanian—and indeed every person in the world that he can reach—as decent, dignified and happy as he possibly can with Jordan's meagre resources.

Today, Christians in Jordan enjoy, by law, 8% of the seats in Parliament and similar quotas at every level of government and society—even though their numbers are less than that in actual fact—in addition to their own personal status laws and Church courts. Their holy sites and legal educational institutes and other needs are safeguarded by the state—and Your Holiness has just seen this in person at the new Catholic University of Madaba, and will, God willing, soon see the new Catholic cathedral and the new Melkite church at the baptism site—and so Christians prosper today in Jordan as they have for the last 2,000 years in peace and harmony, and with goodwill and genuine brotherly relations between them and their Muslim neighbours. This is in part of course because Christians used to be more numerous in Jordan percentage-wise than they are today, but declining Christian birth rates and conversely, high levels of education and prosperity (which has led to their being in demand as immigrants to the West) have reduced their numbers. It is also, however, due to the fact that Jordan appreciates that Christians were in Jordan for 600 years before Muslims. Indeed, Jordanian Christians are perhaps the oldest Christian community in the world—and the majority have always been Orthodox adherents to the Orthodox Patriarchate of Jerusalem and the Holy Land—which, as Your Holiness knows better than I, is the Church of St. James, and was founded during Jesus's own lifetime (may peace be upon him). Many of them are descended from the ancient Arab Ghassanid and Lakhmid Tribes, and they have throughout history shared the fate and the struggles of their Muslim fellow tribesmen. Indeed, in 630 CE during the Prophet Muhammad's own lifetime—may peace and blessings be upon him—they joined the Prophet's own army (led by his adopted son Zeid ibn Al-Haritha and his cousin Jafar bin Abi Taleb) and fought against the Byzantine army of their fellow Orthodox at the Battle of Mutah (it is because of this battle that they earned their tribal name "*'Uzaizat*" which means "the reinforcements"—and the Latin Patriarch Fuad Twal himself comes from these tribes); then in 1099 CE they were slaughtered by Catholic Crusaders at the Fall of Jerusalem alongside their Muslim comrades; later from 1916-1918 CE during the Great Arab revolt they fought against the Muslim Turks alongside their Arab Muslim comrades; they thereafter languished for a few decades along with their Muslim fellows under a Protestant Colonial Mandate, and in the Israeli Arab Wars of 1948, 1967 and 1968 they fought with their Muslim Arab comrades against Jewish opponents. Christian Jordanians have not only always defended Jordan, but have also tirelessly and patriotically helped to build Jordan, playing leading roles in the fields of education, health, commerce, tourism, agriculture, science, culture and many other fields. All this is to say then, that whilst Your Holiness may believe them to be your fellow Christians, we *know* them to be our fellow Jordanians, and they are as much a part of the country as the land itself.

We hope that this unique Jordanian spirit of interfaith harmony, benevolence and mutual respect will serve as an example to the whole world, and that Your Holiness will carry it to places like Mindanao and certain parts of sub-Saharan Africa where Muslim minorities are hard-pressed by Christian majorities, as well as to other places where the opposite is the case.

Now, just as we welcome Your Holiness today in four ways, we receive Your Holiness today in four ways:

First, we receive Your Holiness *as the Spiritual Leader, Supreme Pontiff* and the successor of St. Peter for 1.1 billion Catholics, who are neighbours of Muslims everywhere in the world, and whom we greet through receiving you.

Second, we receive Your Holiness, *as Pope Benedict XVI in particular* whose reign has been marked by the moral courage to do and speak his conscience, no matter what the vogue of the day; who is personally also a master Christian theologian responsible for historical Encyclical Letters on the beautiful cardinal virtues of charity and hope; who has re-facilitated the traditional Latin Mass for those who choose it, and who has simultaneously made intra-faith and inter-faith dialogue a top priority of his reign in order to spread goodwill and understanding throughout all peoples of the world.

Third, we receive Your Holiness *as a Head of State who is also a world and global leader* on the vital issues of morality, ethics, the environment, peace, human dignity, the alleviation of poverty and suffering and even the global financial crisis.

Fourth and finally, we receive Your Holiness as *a simple pilgrim of peace* who comes in humility and gentleness to pray where Jesus Christ, the Messiah—may be peace be upon him—prayed, was baptised and began his mission two thousand years ago.

So welcome to Jordan, Your Holiness Pope Benedict XVI!

God says in the Holy Qur'an to the Prophet Muhammad (may peace and blessings be upon him):

> Glory be to your Lord, the Lord of Might, [exalted is He] above what they allege! / And peace be to the messengers. / And praise be to God, Lord of the Worlds.

(*Al-Saffat*, 37:180-182)

Contributors

David Ford is Regius Professor of Divinity at Cambridge University and Director of the Cambridge Inter-Faith Programme, which is dedicated to engagement with Judaism, Christianity and Islam, with their interrelations, and with their relations to other religions. Recent works include *Christian Wisdom. Desiring God and Learning in Love and The Shape of Theology.*

Ibrahim Kalin is professor of Islamic studies at Georgetown University. His publications include articles on Islamic philosophy and Western perceptions of Islam, and he has translated a number of Islamic philosophical texts from Arabic into English. His book *Islam and the West* (published in Turkish) has won the 2007 Writers Association of Turkey award for best book.

Ghazi bin Muhammad: H.R.H. Prince Ghazi bin Muhammad bin Talal received his BA from Princeton University and his Ph.D From Trinity College, Cambridge University. He serves as Cultural Secretary and Advisor for Tribal Affairs to His Majesty King Abdullah II of The Hashemite Kingdom of Jordan. Professor of philosophy at Jordan University, he is the author of numerous articles and books including *Cultural Treasures of Jordan*. He is the coordinator of *A Common Word Initiative*.

Abdal Hakim Murad is the Shaykh Zayed Lecturer in Islamic Studies at the Faculty of Divinity at the University of Cambridge.

Seyyed Hossein Nasr, internationally renowned author, lecturer, and thinker, is University Professor of Islamic Studies at George Washington University. His numerous books include *The Garden of Truth, The Heart of Islam, Knowledge and the Sacred, Man and Nature*, and *Religion and the Order of Nature*.

Reza Shah-Kazemi is a Research Associate at the Institute of Ismaili Studies in London. Dr. Shah-Kazemi writes on a range of topics from metaphysics and doctrine to contemplation and prayer. He is the author of numerous works including *Paths to Transcendence: According to Shankara, Ibn Arabi, and Meister Eckhart*.

Miroslav Volf is Henry B. Wright Professor of Theology, Yale University Divinity School, and the Founding Director of the Yale Center for Faith and Culture. His recent works include *The End of Memory: Remembering Rightly in a Violent World* and *Free of Charge: Giving and Forgiving in a Culture Stripped of Grace*.

The Very Rev. **Dr. Rowan Williams** was enthroned as the Archbishop of Canterbury in 2003. Long acknowledged internationally as an outstanding theological writer, scholar, and teacher, since becoming archbishop, he has turned his attention increasingly to contemporary cultural and interfaith issues. Among his recent theological writings are *Wrestling with Angels: Conversations in Modern Theology*, *Tokens of Trust: An Introduction to Christian Belief*, and *Grace and Necessity: reflections on art and love*.